D1122038

DATE DUE

MARXISM AND CULTURE

Kennikat Press
National University Publications
Literary Criticism Series

General Editor
John E. Becker
Fairleigh Dickinson University

MARXISM
and
CULTURE

*The CPUSA and Aesthetics
in the 1930s*

LAWRENCE H. SCHWARTZ

National University Publications
KENNIKAT PRESS // 1980
Port Washington, N.Y. // London

To Beverly

Manufactured in the United States of America

Published by
Kennikat Press Corp.
Port Washington, N.Y. / London

Library of Congress Cataloging in Publication Data

Schwartz, Lawrence H, 1947–
    Marxism and culture.

    (National university publications)
    Bibliography: p.
    Includes index.
    1. Communism and culture—United States.
2. Communist aesthetics. 3. Communist Party of the
United States. 4. Communism—United States—1917-
HX523.S45   335.43'0973   79-18972
ISBN 0-8046-9255-6

CONTENTS

ABOUT THE AUTHOR

Lawrence H. Schwartz is an assistant professor of English at Montclair State College in Montclair, New Jersey. He is the author of various articles in *The Nation, Polit,* and the *New York Times.*

PREFACE

This book began as a doctoral dissertation at Rutgers University. There I learned that, irrespective of the quality of my research, it would prove unsatisfactory to the ruling elite's kept experts in cultural and literary history. When one such professor on the dissertation committee rejected my research because I reached conclusions he found politically unacceptable, I also learned that the cultural cold war is still alive. His animus against "Stalinism" made it impossible for him to evaluate my conclusions based on the evidence presented.

Clearly, any discussion of Communism during this period, both in the U.S.S.R. and the U.S.A., is hotly ideological. The central issues raised in this study are more than normally ones in which sharp political disagreements abound, and in which scholarship is inevitably influenced by the political atmosphere. One aspect of my research, though not the principal focus, is the discovery that earlier studies on the question of the Communist line on literature in both the Soviet Union and the United States have been fundamentally wrong.

I do not think it remarkable that the formidable political prejudices and pressures of the cold war period led some scholars into drawing conclusions not according to the available evidence but according to certain preconceptions. Scholars are not immune from the society in which they live. Political prejudices are especially understandable at the various Western institutes for Soviet studies which were originally staffed largely by Russian émigrés whose antipathy toward the U.S.S.R. was powerful. It is probably asking too much to expect these men to be objective about the Soviet Union. In any case, I do not think it remarkable that they were not.

Conventional anti-Communism is a constant part of the discussion on culture and Communism in the 1930s; I found this in the scholarly literature and at Rutgers University. Non-Marxists writing on this question have tried to connect events in the United States to those in the Soviet Union. These bourgeois critics argue that Stalin corrupted Communism in the Soviet Union, corrupt Soviet Communism dominated the Communist International, the misguided and evil Comintern controlled all other Communist Parties (especially the smaller ones such as the CPUSA), and, finally, the "Stalinst-tainted" CPUSA poisoned American intellectual and cultural life. For these critics Stalin and "Stalinism" are the culprits.

Finally, it must be noted that in large part the primary evidence for my analysis is based on the pronouncements of the Party and Party leadership on literary matters. It may be argued that to accept Party statements at face value is piety and not scholarship. However, I do not believe that Communist writers are more likely to lie than others. There is much evidence to show that what they said about literary matters was true, and no evidence to show that they lied. The statements of the Party and Party leadership reflect accurately the reality of the posture of the CPUSA toward literature. The aim of this study is to evaluate Marxist aesthetics on the basis of what Communists did in fact try to do, a question that other scholars choose to ignore.

MARXISM AND CULTURE

ABBREVIATIONS

AWC	American Writers' Congress (first or second)
TC	*The Communist*
CC	Central Committee of the Communist Party of the United States
TCI	*The Communist International*
CIO	Congress of Industrial Organizations
CPSU	Communist Party of the Soviet Union (Bolshevik)
CPUSA	Communist Party of the United States of America
DW	*Daily Worker*
ECCI	Executive Committee of the Communist International
FOSP	Federation of Soviet Writers
Int'l. Lit.	International Literature
IURW	International Union of Revolutionary Writers
JRC	John Reed Clubs
LAW	League of American Writers
NEP	New Economic Policy
NM	*New Masses*
PGFF	Professional Groups for Foster and Ford
TPO	*The Party Organizer*
PR	*Partisan Review*
RAPP	Russian Association of Proletarian Writers
SWG	Screen Writers Guild
VAPP	All-Russian Association of Proletarian Writers
VOAPP	The All-Union Organization of Association of Proletarian Writers
WCF	Workers Cultural Federation
YCL	Young Communist League

INTRODUCTION

This study argues that a Marxist aesthetics is not primarily a theoretical problem but rather one that must be understood as part of the political activity of a Communist Party in a specific historical setting. It therefore challenges the view held by many critics who suggest that Marxism should not be equated with Communism; it also challenges the methodology which suggests that a Marxist aesthetics can be spun purely from theory and can be developed into a grand formula. Instead, the emphasis is on the actual efforts of American Communists, during their most influential period, to integrate literary and cultural issues into their general political work. In the 1930s, of course, the CPUSA's primary activity was trade union organizing, and this dominated the Party's politics in all areas.

My analysis is focused on Party practice in literary affairs; I discuss Party intentions and measure Party success. And while my goal is to offer new historical insight on the CPUSA and literature in the 1930s, it is also to suggest a methodology for treating this problem from a Marxist perspective. Not only does this study consider the development of the Party's literary activity; it also offers an analysis of Soviet socialist realism and a critical review of Marxist aesthetic theory.

Any attempt to offer an interpretation of Communist political activity must not only confront the politics of the 1930s but must also detail its own political bias. And there is in this study a Marxist political premise: the significant intellectual and social Marxist force in the twentieth century is Marxism-Leninism, i.e., Bolshevism. The revolutionary struggles of the past sixty years (especially in the Soviet Union and China) show that class struggle is a real force and that the movement toward socialism has advanced, albeit haltingly and with errors. Because Marxism-Leninism

3

has been successful in overthrowing capitalism and beginning to construct socialism, the study of revolutionary Communist Parties has a value not in some abstract sense but because it traces the shape of history. The Communist Party of the Soviet Union in the 1930s worked to use Marxism-Leninism as a weapon in the class struggle and was, at that time, the leader of the revolutionary socialist movement.

It seems to me perfectly logical and legitimate to look to Marxism-Leninism to formulate an understanding of artistic reality. Therefore, when I speak of Marxist aesthetics, it is in fact an abbreviation for Marxist-Leninist aesthetics. This underlies my belief that such an aesthetics can be generated only by a revolutionary Communist Party in the course of social struggle. The CPUSA was such a mass revolutionary Party in the 1930s. My interest in the American Communist Party is an effort to understand how *active* Communists involved in real social struggle approached culture and literature.

2

The emergence of socially conscious art in the 1930s has been well documented and rather carefully dissected, with obligatory praise of new literary forms, new artists, and new themes. Along with the praise came equally obligatory condemnation of perceived "Stalinism," duplicity, and disingenuousness. Of lasting interest has been the role of Communists and the Communist Party in developing, encouraging, and publicizing such art.[1]

One might well ask how the historical lesson of the CPUSA's involvement with literature and culture in the 1930s should be assessed. This is, of course, a small part of the broader question: What is or should be the relationship of art to politics? For most non-Marxist intellectuals art is and should be apolitical. They view both Communism and fascism as forms of totalitarianism which smother artistic expression and retard the progress of culture. Central to this judgment is the belief that for art to flourish the artist must be "free" to follow his creative impulses. Even the anti-Communist leftists of the 1930s argued this position, claiming that the "Stalinist" policies of the CPUSA reduced art to propaganda and artists to political tools.

For Marxists, however, the historical lesson of the 1930s must be viewed differently. First, the belief that art necessarily flourishes under bourgeois liberal democracy must be revised in favor of an understanding that under capitalism artistic creations are primarily commodities controlled by ruling circles for their benefit. Second, for Marxists art cannot be separated objectively from politics and, therefore, the view that politics intrudes into life and art must be revised; political ideas and consciousness emerge from the class struggle and can and should be assimilated and expressed by artists.

The real tragedy in the cultural work of the CPUSA in the 1930s was not, as is usually argued, the intrusion of politics into literature; it was that the Party did *not* develop a more fully conscious political program for art. The more the revolutionary Communist line was submerged in the latter half of the decade, the bigger, and on the surface more successful, the popular front became. The Party thus decided it was not practical to raise a sharp revolutionary line while fighting fascism and building mass organizations.

Too often the political work of the Party is carefully traced by anti-Communist historians who ultimately dismiss it as valueless, or worse. While critical of the CP effort, this study does not scorn the Party's work but offers instead the beginning of a revision, with the 1930s as object lesson, of the standard belief that politics necessarily defeats art. In my view, the weakness of the 1930s was that Communists devoted too much effort to becoming good reformers. As one historian has said:

... the popular-front left made many vital contributions to American life. Its writers and artists explored the life of the common people, sang their songs, and to an extent brought their stories and aspirations onto the American stage and into the motion pictures. The popular-front left created civil rights groups ... to publicize the plight of the Black American. The popular-front left also fought discrimination against ethnic and national minorities. . . . Above all else, the popular-front left provided the leadership in organizing the mass production unions and in helping to consolidate the New Deal's majority coalition. These achievements were certainly more significant than any made by social liberals alone before or since.[2]

But the Party did not use to full advantage its influence to sustain a Communist involvement in literature. They did much as powerful reformers, but could have done more as strong revolutionaries.

However, their success in literary and cultural life, no matter the limitations, does show that socially conscious art can attract a significant audience in America. My study offers an important base from which other studies may begin to reconsider the theater, Hollywood film making, and other white collar intellectual professions without succumbing to the cold war mythologies about Communism and Stalinism.

This study has not produced an easy formula for linking Communist politics to literature. What has been uncovered is evidence to suggest that the cultural direction of the Party was too often determined primarily in an individual way. Virtually every liberal-to-left viewpoint except for Trotskyism was allowed expression. And intellectual and artistic quibbles and debates very often held center stage. In literary and cultural affairs there was no central Party leadership based on clear political analysis.

3

The first section of the text traces the development of Soviet socialist realism in the early 1930s (the prime historical antecedent for Communist literary activity in the decade) and the American Communists' response to it. The political and organizational changes in the Soviet Union are intensively reviewed as a background (given the outlook of this study) to an understanding of the literary policies of the CPUSA. Only with such a deep study of Soviet policy is it possible actually to test whether the CPUSA was following the "Soviet model" in literary matters.

Six basic questions are posed and answered in this section: (1) Why was the Russian Association of Proletarian Writers (RAPP, 1928–32) suddenly disbanded by official decree in April, 1932? (2) Why was it replaced in 1934 by a new organization, the Writers' Union, and a new slogan, "socialist realism"? (3) What were the organizational, political, and aesthetic implications of socialist realism? (4) Was there a clearly articulated "line" for literature and culture in the Soviet Union? (5) When did this line develop, and was there a coherent pattern to that development? (6) How did American Communists interpret Soviet cultural affairs, and did they take directions from Moscow?

The analysis shows that the end of a narrow, sectarian proletarian phase in Soviet literary affairs occurred well before the mid-decade shift to a united front policy, not as a reflexive response to international conditions. The creation in 1934 of a broad-based writers' union reflected a liberalizing trend in intellectual and artistic matters during a period usually characterized as the beginning of Stalin's dictatorship. In fact, there was no rigid "Stalinist" control over literature in the early 1930s.

In the 1928–34 period literary and cultural matters were peripheral issues in the Soviet Union. Nevertheless, the cultural environment was complex and not reducible to a simple formula. The proletarian line espoused by RAPP did dominate Soviet and international Marxist literature for a short period, reaching its apogee in 1930. However, RAPP had no official Party mandate, and its proletarianism was deemphasized in 1932. It is safe to say that the Party had no line on literature until the promulgation of socialist realism in 1934 at the First Congress of the Union of Soviet Writers.

The creation of a single Writers' Union was not designed at the outset to establish a censorship bureau but represented, in the literary field, a far larger and more important political process of rapprochement between the Party and intelligentsia. The evidence shows that socialist realism was not designed as a theory of aesthetics to which writers were forced to adhere, that it was not a scheme to provide censors with arbitrary checklists for approved themes and characters, and that it was not part of a campaign by Stalin to gain tyrannical and absolute control over all ideological and political theories.

The emergence of Soviet socialist realism was part of a general plan to gain more support for the Party from bourgeois intellectuals by involving them in broad-based organizations of both Party members and reticent fellow travelers—the Writers' Union was but one such group. No doubt the purpose was to convince them to support Party work and, ultimately, to get them to join the Party.

Socialist realism was an organizing tool and not an aesthetic—i.e., not a clear, cogent, and comprehensive guide to literary activity. The practical basis for unity within the Writers' Union was quite liberal and unconfining: sympathy for the building of socialism.

In America the theoretical basis and practical organizing of literary and cultural work diverged sharply in important ways. One cannot explain American literary developments merely as an extension of Soviet policies in the arts; cultural ties to the Soviet Union were superficial at best. The American CP did not reflect or impose a Soviet model on the American scene.

First, most anti-Communist commentators argue that Soviet directives on literary matters were passed to American Communists through the International Union of Revolutionary Writers (IURW)—the literary arm of the Comintern dominated completely by RAPP. Of special significance for this view is the Second International Conference of Revolutionary and Proletarian Writers (1930), known as the Kharkov Conference.

It is true that the Kharkov resolutions on literature were the basis for the proletarian literary work of American Communists—i.e., creating the *New Masses* and the John Reed Clubs. However, the proletarian emphasis in America lasted from 1930 to 1935 and included the first American Writers' Congress. This presents an important anomaly: by the summer of 1934 there existed in the Soviet Union a broad-based writers' union, while the CPUSA was still tied to a set of policies indeed promulgated at the Soviet-dominated Kharkov Conference but by a group (RAPP) which was displaced in 1932. Therefore, the American adherence to the proletarian phase shows an actual lag. The Kharkov resolutions were not "orders from Moscow"; they reflected the orientation of RAPP.

The important progression of events in the Soviet Union climaxing in the August, 1934, Writers' Congress and establishment of the Writers' Union was never detailed or explored by the American Communists. In reference to the Soviet Union, the CPUSA was tied to an obviously outmoded literary policy.

Second, it is often argued that calling an American Writers' Congress in the spring of 1935 and forming a League of American Writers reflected the CPUSA's knee-jerk response to orders from the Soviet Union. This is not supported by the evidence. The Writers' Congress was organized on the basic principles of the Kharkov Conference of 1930, not on the slogan of socialist realism or the model of the 1934 Soviet Writers' Congress.

After the Kharkov Conference in 1930 there is little further evidence to show that either the IURW or the American Party leadership offered significant guidance to coordinate American literary efforts with the Soviet changes. The CPUSA did not understand or interpret the political basis for post-1932 changes in Russian literary life. Ironically (given the traditional literature), there was an unexpectedly low level of Soviet influence on American Communist literary affairs.

4

The second part of the account analyzes in some detail the literary and cultural work of the CPUSA in the 1930s. The central question considered in this section is: What was the actual CPUSA plan or program for culture in general and literature in particular? The discussion is based on Party practice as revealed in meetings and conventions, and in Party newspapers and journals, and is divided into five parts: (1) an overview of the Party approach to intellectuals during the decade; (2) a thorough review of the proletarian phase in America and the Party's relationship to it; (3) an evaluation of the changes in Party practice after the united front, detailing the aesthetics of the popular front period, 1935–39; (4) a synthesis of the Party's proletarian and popular front programs; and (5) a critique of the general political line of the Party, focusing on the shift away from the call to revolution after 1935.

Despite the beliefs of professional anti-Communists, the evidence clearly shows that the Party never articulated an aesthetic or even a literary "line" at any time throughout this period. It certainly did not create proletarian literature, did not supervise its growth, and did not prescribe thematic material to writers. But the Party was interested in a socially conscious art and a politicizing of both the art and the artist.

Exploiting the ravages of the depression and encouraging the increased consciousness of left and liberal writers and artists, the CPUSA helped to legitimize socially conscious art and through it to fight fascism. At the height of its influence on cultural affairs, the CP offered, for example, a cultural page each day in the *Daily Worker* and a magazine devoted to culture in the *Sunday Worker;* it had direct ties to the widely read and highly respected *New Masses,* and it had controlling influence in the League of American Writers. All things considered, this was a positive achievement greater than all other Marxist or left groupings in the U.S.

But the central point remains clear. The Party never offered a conscious political program for its large and influential cultural organizations and supporters as it did for those directly involved in trade union work, anti-racism, and social reform. The direction of cultural work was often set by the whimsical personal preferences of the Party's literary and cultural experts. No formulas were offered; rather, as one anti-Communist leftist critic has suggested, the aesthetic was simply that "the writer should ally himself with the working class and recognize the class struggle as the central fact of modern life."[3]

There may have been tacit agreement on this point, but such a direct command was never issued. In a certain sense, the false notion that the artist must be free to create whatever he wants, with the "democratic" marketplace determining what will be consumed, was quietly accepted, although the Party did ask for some personal involvement in political activities.

In an era of heightened social consciousness increasing numbers of intellectuals and writers became self-proclaimed Marxists; some even joined the Party. Obviously, there were CP members who were intellectuals and artists and who led various cultural organizations. However, the Party's approach to intellectuals and cultural workers was generally haphazard and fuzzy. The Party never considered literary and artistic intellectuals as crucial to the success of socialism in America. The Party accepted intellectuals as middle class petty-bourgeois allies but distrusted them as bourgeois individualists and self-seekers—and seemed to work with them far more opportunistically than with other groups. There never existed a coherent strategy or program underlying the Party involvement with intellectuals.

A clear interpretation of the Party approach to culture and literature requires a critique of the dominant political line in terms of trade union organizing and the building of mass anti-fascist and civil rights organizations. The CPUSA's rejection of the primacy of class struggle during the united front period essentially represented an abandonment of the concept of revolutionary socialism. During the latter half of the 1930s the Party created a distorted category of "people's" culture, a category with no clear class analysis. This approach to culture was an error developing from the Party position in the trade unions, and was certainly not dictated by the Comintern. As was demonstrated in the late 1930s and the following two decades, the power of the ruling elite could not be controlled by reformist appeals and tactics alone. In fact, the bourgeoisie was willing to destroy trade union democracy to crush CP advances within the trade union movement.

The evidence on the Party provided in this second section of my account reveals that it adopted, in the late 1930s and lasting throughout World War 2, a basic outlook indistinguishable from the liberal wing of the.U.S. ruling elite. A critical flaw in the Party's position on the united front was that it failed to create a sophisticated understanding of the nature of state power and the class dictatorship of the bourgeoisie—i.e., to maintain theoretically and practically its critical independence from the reform forces within the New Deal.

The Party came to accept the notion that there was such a thing as a people's democratic culture; it actually sought to create such a culture as part of the struggle. And there was the belief that progress could be made in coalition with the bourgeoisie. This was an illusion. Communism is not the same thing as liberal democracy, and the failure to keep this distinction clear proved costly to the CPUSA. Its trade union base was wiped out and its cultural work tainted.

The Party tried to gain acceptance during the united front period by pushing a popular front line without class politics. In practice this error led to the abandonment of Communism as an identifiable force. Without a clear Communist Party line of a revolutionary nature, the diluted Marxism of the popular front blocked the development of any real Marxist aesthetic.

5

The third and concluding segment of the book contrasts the specific historical case study of the CPUSA with the three most basic tendencies in Marxist aesthetic theory. The central criticism of these three approaches is directed at their attempt to create a universal Marxist aesthetic formula based on abstract and impractical theoretical equations and ahistorical evidence.

The three tendencies are: (1) isolating the scattered "dicta" of Marx and Engels and converting them into a complete theory of aesthetics; (2) assuming a mechanical and linear connection between the economic base and the ideological (in this case, literary) superstructure; and (3) placing judgments about art in a variety of sociological, ideological, and dialectical contexts which are presumed a priori to be materialist conventions. These tendencies (based on representative texts) are analyzed to demonstrate the problem of over-theorizing. The fundamental weakness in trying to postulate a grand Marxist aesthetic is the failure to consider the actual work of Communists. The intellectual debate over Marxist aesthetics is usually carried on far removed from practice, and my research shows the need for careful historical analysis of active Communist Parties.

6

A prefatory remark about Stalin and Stalinism is warranted. The opening chapter confronts directly and consciously the problem of Stalin and historical accuracy. It will be obvious that the position taken repudiates the central thrust of most scholarship, both anti- and pro-Marxist. However, I believe that it is necessary to consider Stalin outside of the tautological, tendentious, and tiresome role of the supreme and maniacal dictator. I suggest that, to gain a clear perception of cultural matters in the Soviet Union during this period, one must try to suspend the usual vision of Stalin and assess the evidence objectively.

To see this period in the Soviet Union primarily as the building of Stalin's dictatorship distorts the reality that the leadership in Russia was Communist. Stalin and other Party leaders made errors, but these errors were made by Marxist-Leninists, not by robot-like stooges of an evil tyrant. Frankly, a central assertion underlying my analysis of socialist realism is that the Soviet Union in the 1930s was not yet a dictatorship in the traditional sense—i.e., one-man rule.

The famous purge trials of the mid-thirties are not treated because there is no evidence from the trials or from the documents released in the post-1956 era of de-Stalinization which indicates that the promulgation of socialist realism and the reorganizing of writers' groups was part of Stalin's plan to eliminate opposition and consolidate power. My research shows quite clearly that the issue of the purge trials has no relevance to the study of the reorganization of writers' groups in the early thirties. Furthermore, I believe that inclusion of a discussion of these purge trials would be obeisance to yet another myth of the cold war which would have us believe that it is not possible to discuss any phenomenon in the Soviet Union in the late-1920s and 1930s without consideration of the purges.

How Communists decided to approach literature is the subject of this study. An analysis of socialist realism alone will not provide incontrovertible evidence that Stalin was not the omniscient dictatorial pretender many critics would have us believe. And a study of the CPUSA literary policy alone will not refute the contention that the American Party was bound inextricably to the demands of the Comintern. But it can make a significant advance in debunking the cold war mythology that portrayed everything Communist as the work of diabolical and mechanical monsters.

Finally, much of the analysis in this book is highly critical of Communist practice in both the Soviet Union and the United States. However, it proceeds from a belief that there were significant positive achievements. The legacy from this period is a vital Marxist literature and cultural theory showing the strength of the masses. In the Soviet Union the Party promoted both literature and literacy; art had a specific social function, reflecting the political struggle of the masses to achieve socialism. In America writers and artists associated with the CP or influenced by its politics produced art of enduring value; it endures because it is socially conscious art and attacks the elite and elitist values.

PART 1

SOVIET SOCIALIST REALISM

CHAPTER 1

THE STALIN MYTH
AND SOVIET CULTURE

A clear understanding of the Soviet approach to culture and literature in the 1930s has been obscured by the politics and mythology of the cold war. In the 1930s the central theme of the Soviet approach to literature is usually characterized by the term "socialist realism." This term as popularly used by non-Marxists suggests that socialist realism is a proscriptive aesthetic in which the artist is confined to depicting in didactic and graphic terms the struggle to build socialism.[1] From this perspective, aesthetic and ideological guidance is provided by the Party through its literary bureaucracy—the Writers' Union created in 1934. In this popular sense, socialist realism is both a literary method and a political tool, and the Party's intentions are to control both the writer and the literary product. Socialist realism therefore becomes a euphemism for the political control of literature and carries many negative implications—regimentation, bureaucratization, and stifling of creativity. While this may be the popular view, it oversimplifies an exceedingly complex cultural and political milieu.

The direction of the CPSU in its approach to literature and culture is a key factor in interpreting the program of the CPUSA in literary affairs. If there was a clear line within the Soviet Union, to what extent was it imposed or imitated by American Communists? If one accepts non-Marxists who simplify the question, the guidance provided by the Soviet Union was immediately adopted by the subservient Americans. However, a satisfying analytical view of socialist realism has so far been obscured by cold war scholarship, with all the ideological and polemical encumbrances which such scholarship entails.

There is also a more general problem: "Stalinism." A vast body of material exists which portrays Soviet society after 1929 as dominated by the "dictator" Stalin. It is not unwarranted to suggest that most non-Marxian scholarship takes the view that Stalin ruled the Soviet Union as a one-man dictatorship—creating a totalitarian regime. At the same time, much Marxist scholarship based on Khrushchev era (1956-65) sources sees Stalin's rule as despotic and an aberration in the development of Socialism.

Such interpretations may be seen in Merle Fainsod's *How Russia Is Ruled* (1953, 1963) and Adam Ulam's *Stalin: The Man and His Era* (1973), representing non-Marxist/Western scholarship, and in Roy A. Medvedev's *Let History Judge: The Origins and Consequences of Stalinism* (1971), representing Marxist but not official Soviet scholarship. Fainsod writes:

Stalin erected a structure of centralized, absolute authority in which un-questioned obedience to his dictates became a *sine qua non* of survival. He ruthlessly eliminated every actual or potential competitor for supreme power and encouraged the development of a leadership cult in which his own godlike infallibility served as an object of official worship. He de-veloped a system of competing and overlapping bureaucratic hierarchies in which both the Party and the police, penetrating and watching each other, simultaneously pervaded and controlled the armed forces, the administration, and all other organized sectors of life. He reserved his own ultimate authority to direct and coordinate the system by providing no point to final resolution for differences and conflicts short of himself.

The art of successful totalitarian dictatorship as it evolved under Stalin required a capacity to gauge the endurance of its subjects. . . . While never abandoning the substance of his authority and steadily extending his con-trol of the key power positions in the Soviet state, he also demonstrated considerable skill in interrupting his march toward total power by periodic concessions and breathing spaces. By apparent reversals of policy, he gained time to consolidate his position and to reclaim support which earlier policies had alienated. He showed himself adept at diverting blame to his subordinates for mistakes and difficulties while reserving credit to himself for all major achievements and acts of clemency.

As Stalinism entered its mature phase of totalitarian development, its institutional characteristics tended to harden. The police, military, and administrative apparatuses took on the character of rigid, bureaucratic hierarchies with a paraphernalia of titles, ranks, uniforms, and insignia reminiscent of Tsarist political arrangements.[2]

Fainsod's thesis expresses the view that after 1929, with Trotsky ex-pelled and the right opposition defeated, Stalin was left in "undisputed control." He not only created a cult of personality but also developed a bureaucratic hierarchy at all levels of society which were subject to his direction though also operating as "centers of influence in their own right." This view is repeated in Ulam's recent biography, especially in the lengthy chapter entitled "The War against the Nation." Robert Slusser, in his review of the Ulam work, notes the connection to Fainsod.

For Ulam, Stalin after 1929 was essentially what he had been before: the ablest, shrewdest, most ruthless of the Bolshevik leaders. Following this approach Ulam sets forth what can be described as an updated, more sophisticated version of the concept of Stalinism that was presented in Merle Fainsod's classic study. . . . For Fainsod Stalin after 1929 was the unchallenged leader of a party and a nation that had been thoroughly subdued. Evidence incompatible with this concept—for example, indications of a link between the deputy secret police chief Yagoda and the Right Opposition—was either ignored or minimized.
    Ulam is too well informed a scholar simply to repeat Fainsod's approach—by now the evidence pointing to a continuing internal opposition to Stalin after 1929 is too well established to be ignored. But Ulam still sees the controversial episodes of Stalin's career after 1929 from the old viewpoint; for him Stalin's position was never in jeopardy, nor was there ever any serious attempt to limit his power.[3]

The problem of dictatorship and totalitarianism is handled far differently in Marxist scholarship. For example, in Medvedev's widely heralded study the issue is seen as an aberration. The editor of the English language edition, David Joravsky, explains Medvedev's approach:

The Soviet audience for which this book was written would take for granted things that may puzzle or annoy outsiders. Stalinism itself is a term that may cause confusion, for many people in the West have only a vague notion of the difference between Stalinism and the Soviet system of Communism in general. Medvedev draws a sharp distinction. He uses Stalinism to mean personal despotism sustained by mass terror and by worship of the despot ("the cult of the personality"), precisely those features of the Soviet system that Stalin's successors repudiated, sometimes calling them crimes but usually brushing them off as "mistakes." Medvedev agrees with the official view in one sense: he regards despotism and terror and the cult as accidental deformations of a fundamentally sound system, mistakes on the part of the Party and the country as a whole. He vehemently denies that they were mistakes on Stalin's part, for Stalin deliberately engineered them. They must be listed among Stalin's crimes, not among his mistakes.[4]

Christopher Hill, in his joint review of Ulam and Robert Tucker's *Stalin as Revolutionary, 1879-1929* (1973) points to a central difficulty in trying to deal with Stalin and Stalinism: in addition to evidence there are myths and counter-myths which must be confronted and understood.

To write a biography of Stalin must be a daunting task. It is difficult to write impartially about any revolutionary leader. Revolutions generate myths, and any historian is likely to take an attitude, favorable or hostile, to the achievements of the revolution in which his hero participated. In the case of very recent history, it is difficult not to have prejudices of one's own—about Hitler or Mussolini, Roosevelt or Churchill—quite apart from the prejudiced nature of some of the evidence. But these are problems which normally face the historian—sifting evidence, discounting personal distortions. Most of the evidence is available: all that remains is to check it and interpret it.

In the case of Stalin the evidence itself is elusive. It has been subject not to one mythmaking process but to several. . . . Two myths—at least—emerged: the Stalinist myth of the lives of Stalin and Trotsky, and the Trotskyist myth. Both myths were rewritten as political circumstances changed. Then after Stalin's death in 1953 and the decision to end "the cult of personality" there came the Khrushchev myth of Stalin.[5]

The presence of this mythology on initial premises and interpretation of evidence is significant. It is both a question of duration and of intensity. At least the first two decades of scholarship on Stalin rely heavily on Trotsky's observations. Stalin's brilliant political rival influenced both Marxist and non-Marxist scholars but he is no longer considered a primary source. In reviewing this tendency to rely on Trotsky, the historian Robert H. McNeal observed: "Rarely has the historical image of a major leader been shaped as much by his arch-enemy as the generally accepted conception of Stalin has been shaped by the writings of Trotsky."[6]

After Stalin's death in 1953 the cult of personality was repudiated, and with Khrushchev's secret speech to the Twentieth Party Congress there began an official anti-Stalin campaign which led to an expansive literature within the Soviet Union and in the West. This phase lasted until 1965 when the official position on Stalin softened under Brezhnev and Kosygin, although sharp attacks on Stalin emerged from the *samizdat* groups and individual dissidents. On the Khrushchev myth, Christopher Hill writes:

To this we owe a great deal of information previously unavailable, but it has to be used with caution. Khrushchev had his own political axe to grind, his own skeletons to keep locked up in cupboards. The infallibility of Lenin was still an article of faith, so that exaggerated significance was attached to relations with him. In consequence of all this the revelations were incomplete, one-sided, and need almost as much interpretation as the Stalinist and Trotskyist myths. Finally, in the last few years the

Soviet regime, recognizing the difficulties of letting half a cat out of a bag, has tried to discourage further discussions. A great many essential facts about Stalin's life (and death) are still totally unknown.[7]

What presents itself in much of the literature on Stalin is a combination of a "great man" theory and a concept of totalitarianism too much shaped by the tensions of the cold war. As Roger Pethybridge, a well-known British sovietologist, recently commented:

If one considers all the well-known biographies of Stalin, a common feature emerges: the volumes are a quite accurate reflection of biographical method current at the end of the nineteenth and the beginning of the twentieth centuries, when historical biographies dwelt on so-called "good" and "bad" kings. The personality who reigned appeared to dominate not only the political but the social and economic life of his kingdom, so that by a sneeze or a yawn he could magically change the whole socioeconomic pattern of his reign. This method of historical biography has long been discounted in the treatment of authoritarian rule in earlier history. It has also been discarded with regard to the study of Nazi Germany. Unfortunately, it still remains as a specter from the past in the study of Soviet personalities in high politics.[8]

Hopefully, the scholarship on Stalin can and will move beyond the mechanistic view of the omniscient dictator. This is not a call to ignore evidence of repression and totalitarianism, but it is a call to reject hypotheses which suggest that all events in the Soviet Union were tied irrevocably to Stalin's will.[9]

For example, in a recent article Sheila Fitzpatrick of the Russian Institute at Columbia University and a leading scholar on cultural matters in the Soviet Union during the 1920s and 1930s suggests that the "totalitarian" (a term that is imprecise to begin with) model which has come to dominate non-Marxist scholarship is really a description of the late Stalin period of 1946–53. This is the era of Andrey Zhdanov's dominance and of harsh and rigid controls over culture labeled in the scholarly literature as *zhdanovshchina*—although he died in 1948.

Fitzpatrick suggests that "once the concept of 'full totalitarianism' had been established for the period of 1946–53, the previous years of Soviet power were interpreted accordingly as development toward totalitarianism." In Fitzpatrick's view, most non-Marxist scholarship is based on the belief that the Party wanted absolute control and Stalin wanted full control of the Party; therefore, "the party controlled culture and Stalin controlled the party." She describes four basic assumptions involved in this scholarly approach:

(1) that the party assumed responsibility for guiding, and if necessary forcing, scholarship and the arts in certain directions, generally directions suggested by ideology; (2) that Stalin required an identifiable "party line" on all cultural questions, and thereby excluded the possibility of fundamental debate within the cultural professions; (3) that the Stalinist party rejected even limited concepts of professional autonomy and academic and artistic freedom which had been accepted under NEP, and by imposing total control deprived cultural institutions and professional organizations of all powers of initiative and negotiations; (4) that, as a consequence, there was a "we-they" relationship between the cultural intelligentsia and the party, with the party striving—usually successfully—to infuse its values into the intelligentsia.[10]

Fitzpatrick is not denying the validity of this viewpoint but she is concerned that there may be a reading back: Are scholars using a model of the later period with its sharp censorship, zealous adulation of Stalin, and coercion of intellectuals to explain all of the Stalin era? She further writes: "The totalitarian model was created under the impact of postwar developments which struck Western observers as sinister and appalling. . . . Interpretation of the Soviet system was based on extrapolation back into the past and forward into the future from this focal point."[11]

The impact of the totalitarian schema on the scholarship addressing culture in general and socialist realism in particular has been significant. The imprint of this model is most clearly seen in the general non-Marxist Soviet literary histories that appear in the West. Perhaps the smoothest and most comprehensive of the general surveys of Soviet literature is Gleb Struve's *Russian Literature under Lenin and Stalin, 1917-1953* (1970). It is readable and more heavily documented than most general texts. This analysis is based on the third revision of his literary history, which first appeared as *Soviet Russian Literature* (1935).

Simply stated, Struve's view of Communist political intervention in literature is negative. He believes that socialist realism was designed as a technique to guarantee that literature become "a docile instrument of Party policy." The shift to socialist realism in the 1932-34 period, he explains, was part of a series of far-reaching changes inaugurated by Stalin to insure the preservation of "the totalitarian single party dictatorship." These were for Struve the watershed years marking the complete shift to the cult of Stalin:

It was in the thirties that the Soviet Union became the thorough-going totalitarian state it is now. Viewed retrospectively, the literary "reform" of 1932, which did away with proletarian and other organizations and set up a homogeneous writers' organization pledged to support the domestic and international policies of the Soviet government, was a clever step in the direction of suppressing all nonconformism and establishing a totalitarian control over all manifestations of spiritual and cultural life.[12]

In tracing the literary history of the 1918 to 1934 period, Struve suggests four distinct phases. The first period (War Communism, 1918–22) is characterized primarily by the hostility of the older writers and the confused environment in which older strains of Russian literature (Symbolism, Imagism, and Futurism) were confronted and changed by the revolution. This was also the initiating period for the *proletkult* movement.

With the civil war over, the second period (New Economic Policy, 1922–28) is marked by resurgence of literary activity. Many new publishing enterprises were started, new magazines began publication, and the novel returned as the primary literary voice with the revolution as the dominant theme. It was a period of intense critical controversies between proletarian and non-proletarian groups. The non-Communist sympathizers became known in this period as fellow travelers, Trotsky's famous label. Also during NEP there appeared the first major pronouncement on literature by the Central Committee (June 1925). Struve characterizes the resolution as stipulating a policy of "benevolent encouragement" toward non-Communist writers:

In a way the 1925 resolution of the Central Committee merely sanctioned the existing order of things. Its importance lay in the fact that the claim of proletarian literary organizations to play the leading role in literature and to control the literary production of non-Communists was firmly rejected. Fellow travelers were given more elbow room and enabled to continue their work in peace. . . .
The period during which the principles of the 1925 resolution governed literary life in the Soviet Union proved to be rich and fruitful.[13]

The third period (the first Five-Year Plan, 1929–32) is dominated according to Struve by a distinct shift in the official attitude toward literature. The free and easy environment of NEP with its competing literary elements ended with the Russian Association of Proletarian Writers (RAPP) gaining a controlling position. He writes:

The period of comparative freedom was at an end, and to it succeeded what came to be known as the dictatorship of the RAPP, which was headed unofficially by the most virulent of critics, Leopold Averbakh. This period lasted about three years and coincided with the early years of the First Soviet Five-Year Plan of industrialization and collectivization, to which everything else in the country was subordinated. Literature, too, was enlisted in its service. The leading role in it was given to Communist writers and purely "proletarian" organizations. RAPP assumed dictatorial powers and laid down the policy which all writers had to follow if they cared to survive in literature.[14]

Finally, there is the fourth period (Socialist Realism, 1932-34). For Struve the 1932 Central Committee decision to dissolve RAPP was the most important of the entire 1918 to 1932 era.

In substance it meant the disbanding of all proletarian (and other) literary organizations and the creation, in their place, of a single Union of Soviet Writers. This step was motivated by "the achievements of Socialist Construction," which made the existence of separate proletarian literary and artistic organizations superfluous. The party decided that, having succeeded in breaking in literature and subordinating it to its plan, it had achieved a sufficient degree of homogeneity which could be maintained in future.

This reversal of policy meant doing away with the very conception of fellow travelers. For some time the more moderate among the Communist writers and critics had been insisting that it was wrong to lump all fellow travelers together—that those who were known under this name could really be divided into two main groups: (1) enemies of the Revolution, whether open or disguised, and (2) allies.

. . . .

It can be seen then, that behind the Central Committee's "historic" decision lay not so much the concern for the writers' and artists' freedom as the realization that Averbakh's tactics of dictatorial regimentation of art were not bearing fruit and that other methods had to be tried to ensure that literature should follow the party line, without at the same time impairing its quality.[15]

The pattern which Struve describes shows that as the Communists stabilize their control, literature becomes more regimented and circumscribed. His equation is linear: the stronger the Communist regime, the fewer the freedoms. The periods of competition and freedom (i.e., War Communism and NEP) were fruitful and productive, while the periods of control and censorship (RAPP and Socialist Realism) were inhibiting and debilitating. For Struve the fellow travelers Fedin, Leonov, Kaverin, Slonimsky, Olesha, A. Tolstoy, Prishvin, and Ehrenburg "made the greatest contribution to Soviet literature from 1924 to 1929." In his view, the revival of literature in this period came to an end in 1929 when the fellow travelers and independents were harshly criticized by RAPP. He sees literature being subordinated to the requirements of the Five-Year Plan "with results that were disastrous to Soviet literature as a whole." This negative turn was further exacerbated by the 1932 decision to form a single Union of Soviet Writers:

This step was designed primarily to put an end to factional squabbles and to create a body that would be more or less homogeneous, held together by officially approved bylaws and hence more easily controllable. The union was to comprise all Soviet writers who accepted the general policy of the Soviet government, supported Socialist reconstruction, and adhered in their work to the method of Socialist Realism. . . . However ill-defined may have been this method . . . its use circumscribed the writer's scope by imposing on him the obligation to deal in his work with "Socialist realities." By the very act of adhering to the Union of Soviet Writers . . . a Soviet writer limited the range of his creative work of his own accord and agreed to serve the Soviet State and its ultimate policies in his capacity as a writer.[16]

Struve sees this 1932 decision as a clear tightening of control and reduction of freedom that had been granted in 1925. For him, homogeneity was a euphemism for domination—"complete compliance of the writers with the demands made on them by the party." He is particularly upset by the intrusion of politics into literature:

The political factor remained decisive, and although writers were no longer expected to write purely industrial or political novels, they were expected to adhere to Socialist Realism or face ostracism. The Union of Soviet Writers was thus a typical by-product of a totalitarian regime. It was not an ordinary professional organization, for all its members were not only obliged to subscribe to a definite political program but also tied down to a specific literary method.[17]

The four-part division which Struve isolates has become the standard method of treating Soviet literature in this period. However, one notices that post–World War 2 overviews and general texts tend to be harsher in their judgments about regimentation and control, while many written in the 1930s were more sympathetic.[18] For example, in an introduction to a collection of Soviet writing published in 1933, George Reavey and Marc Slonim, both well-known literary historians, take a view that the April 1932 decision to dissolve RAPP seems to be a shift to a more liberal policy and not a new approach to regiment literature:

It became perfectly obvious that the attempt at a literary Five-Year Plan was threatening to disintegrate Soviet Literature. . . . The discontent of writers . . . assumed such serious proportions that the Soviet government was forced to grant another Charter of Liberation. The revolution that followed must be attributed in great measure to the interference of Gorky and to the decision of Stalin, who had become irritated at the poor results of the Communist drive in art and literature.

. . . .

But whereas the Central Committee Resolution of 1925 had legalized a situation which had arisen out of the literary dispute of the time and had given the Fellow Travelers their full "citizenrights," the April decree brought about an "organic" revolution. The RAPP was dissolved and the literary dictatorship brought to an end. The uncompromising policy of the extremist was definitely condemned and Soviet writers were invited to join a general "Association of Soviet Writers," within which the Communist writer would form their own faction.[19]

Reavey, in a short overview of Soviet literature written in 1947, became somewhat suspicious of the Writers' Union established in 1934: "The Union, however, like all similar organizations of the post–1932 period, had its simple and effective controls subtly interwoven into the fabric of the whole as part of the administrative machinery."[20] And in terms of the 1932 dissolution of RAPP and the subsequent creation of the union, he still does not see it as evidence of dictatorship:

This was one of the fundamental literary reforms of the 1930s and created a basis of unity among writers, which had not previously existed when it was a question of proletarian writers versus the rest or of other conflicting movements. By the new measure equal status was granted to all and by 1934, when the first All-Union Congress was held, attended by the representatives of 52 Soviet nationalities, and when reports on 23 national literatures were read, a common platform was worked out on the principle of Socialist Realism.[21]

However, a noticeable change occurred in 1964 when Slonim published *Soviet Russian Literature: Writers and Problems.* Here the tone was vitriolic, condemning Communist control of literature and now sharply attacking the 1932 decision. Slonim saw the attempt at unity of Soviet literature under a single union as artificial:

The Union of Soviet Writers later became not only a professional organization but a powerful political body, ruled by officials who received their instructions from the Party, sometimes from Stalin himself. . . . "The most important consequence, however, of the 1932 change was the decision of the Kremlin to formulate its own literary doctrine, partly on the suggestion of Gorky, partly as developed by Stalin and other Communist leaders. This was the so-called 'socialist realism.' " . . . But instead of applying a purely political criterion (which at bottom was their sole preoccupation), they tried to disguise it in a pseudo-literary formula.
. . . .
When at the convention of the Union of Soviet Writers in 1934, the delegates approved the formula of socialist realism presented by Andrey Zhdanov, the Party spokesman, they could hardly foresee all the implica-

tions and complications of this vote. The overwhelming majority in favor of the formula should not deceive the literary historian. It was a political not a literary near-unanimity.[22]

In Slonim's later argument he cites the 1932 decision as the beginning of the subjugation of literature to politics—i.e., unity really meant uniformity. Having all the writers under the auspices of a single organization made it easier, in Slonim's view, to control literature.

Perhaps the most strident example of the non-Marxist condemnation of political intervention in literary matters is Max Hayward and Leopold Labedz, editors, *Literature and Revolution in Soviet Russia 1917-1962: A Symposium*. In Max Hayward's introduction to the collection he explains the purpose of the essays: "A study of the Party's attempt to impose its will on literature and the arts is interesting in a general sense for students of totalitarian politics. In this field . . . it has been a question of trying to impose a total doctrinal and administrative discipline on a form of human activity which depends entirely on highly individual skills."[23]

Perhaps the most articulate non-Marxist discussion of Soviet control over literature is Harold Swayze's *Political Control of Literature in the USSR, 1946-1959*. His focus is primarily on the post-war Zhdanov period but reaches back to the 1930s for the roots of the modern totalitarianism in the realm of literature. He sees in the early Stalin period the domination of politics over literature: "The theory that politics has a profound impact on literature has become the thesis that politics is the essence of literature." He points to the 1932 dissolution of RAPP and Zhdanov's speech at the 1934 Writers' Congress as sources of control:

. . . Although the Central Committee's decree of that year purported to be a step toward liberalization . . . it is evident that the impulse of the decree was in precisely the opposite direction. The decree was the expression of an urge toward uniformity, and it created an instrument to generate that condition—a single writers' organization under direct party supervision, an organization to supplant all existing independent literary groups.[24]

His conclusions are direct and tough:

. . . the Communist Party has set out to harness literary forces to the service of specific political tasks while limiting and controlling the range of influences . . . that literary works may have. For it is precisely the qualities which render literature useful to the regime as an instrument that make it a potential danger as well.

. . . .

... the Soviet regime has elaborated a literary doctrine and developed practical devices to confine imagination and creativeness within specified compartments. But this activates forces which tend to weaken the affective powers of literature and to reduce its usefulness as an instrument of social control. Maintaining a balance between these contrary tendencies is a central problem of Soviet literary politics.[25]

While Swayze provides a useful analysis for the Zhdanov period, one must be skeptical of its application to an earlier time, especially without corroborating evidence. Swayze is exemplary of Western non-Marxist scholars who are hostile to what they see as the politicization of literature. Such interpretations emanate primarily from the academic centers of Russian studies in the United States where the now universally accepted notion of Stalin as dictator was packaged for academic circles.

The discussions of socialist realism align with the dictator hypothesis, namely that the imposition of socialist realism was one part of the program to increase control and to insure censorship in all social and political affairs marking Stalin's rise to power. These interpretations assume that there was a deliberate regimentation of literature and art to force obeisance to the political line of the Party; and furthermore, that with the aid of his political henchmen, unwilling writers were compelled to participate in the single Writers' Union formed in 1934 to inaugurate and control the "new method" (socialist realism) in literature.

Essentially, these scholars see socialist realism as a "phony" aesthetics with roots in politics and not in art and creativity. The organization of a single Writers' Union guided by socialist realism in art marks the complete subservience of art to politics. For these interpreters socialist realism both as an artistic method and a technique of organization is little more than Stalinist dictatorship over literary affairs—i.e., censorship and control.

As we shall see in the next chapter, when socialist realism is considered outside the context of the totalitarian model it becomes part of a broad effort to enlist the support of bourgeois elements (intellectuals, professionals, scientists, writers, etc.) who at the outset of the revolution were often the least cooperative or even the most hostile. The effort at rapprochement required organizational changes deemphasizing the proletarian theme of the First Five-Year Plan. The position taken in the next chapter suggests that the general line of the Party was to make large concessions to the bourgeoisie—essentially to form a united front very much in the style of the post-1935 era—to gain their support. In the realm of literature this shift results in the organizing of a single Writers' Union to provide writers with expanded material support and preferential treatment.

CHAPTER 2

FROM PROLETARIANISM TO SOVIET SOCIALIST REALISM

There is little disagreement about the literary developments in the 1920s during the NEP period from 1922 to 1928 which form the background to socialist realism. Cultural policy during NEP was dominated not by the Party but by various government agencies. There was of course censorship and control within the Communist framework, but the broad Party policy was to encourage support from the "bourgeois specialists." And in the cultural arena responsibility fell nominally to Lunacharsky's Narkompros, the Commissariat of Enlightenment.[1]

The proletarian literary movement that eventually developed into RAPP began in December 1922 when a group of young and aggressive Communists broke with an older writers' organization (the Smithy) over acceptance of NEP. They met in the editorial offices of the Komsomol magazine *Young Guard,* then edited by the teenager Leopold Averbakh, who later became the leader of RAPP. The group called itself "October" and was composed of young writers who saw the need for a mass proletarian literary organization. They came essentially from middle class intellectual backgrounds and had fought as adolescents in the Red Army. This October group, affecting a military style and proletarian outlook, came to control VAPP, the All-Russian Association of Proletarian Writers; the principal leaders were S. Rodov, G. Levelich, and I. Vardin.

In their journal *On Guard* they advocated direct Party intervention in literary matters to support the idea of proletarian culture. These young proletarians were very much concerned with ideology and the politics of literature. Their sharply proletarian stand and their "hard" line on Communist vigilance ran counter to the prevailing openness of NEP and into direct confrontation with the leading literary figure of the early twenties, Alexander Voronsky, editor of the influential Communist magazine *Red Virgin Soil*.[2] Voronsky was attacked by October for his sympathetic approach to fellow travelers and his rejection of a strictly proletarian culture. However, Voronsky had the support of many influential Party and government leaders, including Lunacharsky and Mesheriakov, head of the State Publishing House.

The antagonisms between Voronsky and VAPP ultimately led to a Central Committee resolution entitled "On the Policy of the Party in the Field of Belles Lettres" (July 1, 1925). Written primarily by Bukharin, the resolution was an ambiguous document. It was used by both sides in the debate to justify their positions. Basically, it called for the support of fellow travelers and assistance to proletarians. While recognizing the ultimate hegemony of the proletarian approach to culture, VAPP was *not* given official Party endorsement as leader in literary affairs. The resolution reiterated the guiding theme of NEP: free competition among opposing literary groups. The resolution was carefully designed not to alienate either side.[3]

However, Voronsky continued to be attacked after the 1925 resolution and was eventually forced out as editor of *Red Virgin Soil*. There was a consistent effort by his critics (VAPP included) to tie him both to Trotsky's theoretical positions and to the active oppositionists.

The resolution also created changes within VAPP. Vardin, Rodov, Levelich, and their followers resisted the resolution. When the Central Committee's press department was given the responsibility for organizing a Federation of Soviet Writers (FOSP) which was to include both proletarian and fellow traveler groups, the Vardin leadership resisted. The wrangling over this issue gave Averbakh's group control. The Vardin group, holding to its "left" position (i.e., resisting cooperation with non-Communist writers), was excluded from the leadership though it remained in the organization. Although Averbakh's group tried to align closely to the Party, it still held to the proletarian position demanding that the Party be active in support of the Communist literary movement and calling for stronger censorship and greater "proletarian dictatorship." They wanted Communist control of cultural institutions. However, until 1928 they received virtually no active support from anyone in the higher Party leadership. More importantly, they *never* received the mandate to set literary policy in the name of the Party.[4]

The NEP period ended dramatically with the Shakhty trial in the spring of 1928, when fifty-five mining engineers and technicians in the Shakhty area of Donbass were accused of sabotage. This marked the opening of a general class war on the cultural front. The bourgeois specialists were now under suspicion, leaving the way open for the young Communists and proletarians to assume more power and authority. The proletarian phase in culture and its attendant cultural revolution lasted in literature until April 1932, when RAPP and the other cultural proletarian organizations were dissolved by Central Committee mandate.

In 1928, at the All-Union Congress of Proletarian Writers, VAPP was reorganized and became RAPP. Also at this Congress the proletarians began to get official endorsement with supporting speeches by Lunacharsky, Krinitsky (member of the Central Committee), and Lazian, secretary of the Moscow Party Committee. The proletarian emphasis commencing with the Shakhty affair was what the young Communists in RAPP had been demanding, and they struggled during the next three years to gain official sanction while trying to solidify the proletarian position in literary and cultural organizations.

Traditionally, the rise and fall of RAPP is explained in terms of deepening repression and control of literature by the Party. It becomes another part of the "totalitarian" hypothesis of a "Stalinist dictatorship" suggesting a conscious plan to subvert literature through careful orchestration by the Party. One explanation of RAPP's dissolution argues that it resisted the effort of the Party to use literature directly as an instrument of policy. In this view, RAPP while working under the guidance of the Party was too independent and somewhat averse to the utilitarian approach to literature. RAPP is seen in this context as an entity distinct from the Party because RAPP continued a policy of proletarian exclusiveness at a time when the Party was shifting (after 1931) to a more favorable attitude toward fellow travelers and bourgeois specialists.[5]

A second traditional interpretation suggests that RAPP was dissolved because it was not suited to the Party's need for even more rapid and complete imposition of ideological and artistic uniformity. Here RAPP is seen as a Party instrument which helped to cut off the critical debates and the competition between conflicting theories of NEP. RAPP survived until 1932 because it was in accord with Party policy and helped the Party suppress artistic dissent; its orthodoxy and obedience during Stalin's theoretical proletarian offensive guaranteed its continuance. In this view, the dissolution of RAPP in 1932 and the formation of a single writers' union in 1934 under the slogan of socialist realism was the culmination of a trend leading to the complete domination of the Party over literary affairs.[6]

Recently a number of Western scholars have begun to reevaluate Soviet cultural activities in the crucial 1928–32 period, breaking away from the totalitarian model. These scholars argue that the proletarian period may best be understood as an episode in cultural revolution with all the attendant upheavals and dislocations associated with the contemporary use of the term.[7] In the realm of culture, it was fundamentally a class war between "proletarian" Communists and "bourgeois" intelligentsia. This is in opposition to the traditional interpretation which contends that class war terminology was little more than a smokescreen for Party regimentation of the intelligentsia during the transition from NEP to the Stalin dictatorship. Sheila Fitzpatrick explains:

The scholarship has been largely focused on the persecution of the old intelligentsia and the extension of political controls over cultural life. It has treated the First Five-Year Plan period as a transition, arbitrarily and abruptly separating the NEP period of relative tolerance and cultural diversity from the Stalin period of repression and cultural stagnation. The Party, or Stalin himself, has often been seen holding the levers of change and manipulating them almost at will to reach preconceived goals.
. . . .
. . . we have made the first attempt to see the cultural revolution as a whole, and to consider it not simply as a transition but as a discrete phenomenon with its own special characteristics. Instead of concentrating exclusively on the theme of Party intervention in culture (the major theme of previous Western studies), we have looked at what was happening *within* the cultural professions. . . .[8]

According to Sheila Fitzpatrick, the period of class war cultural revolution was a mixture of revolution from above and below. In part, the Party leadership used the cultural revolution in its general campaign against the right, but it was always a peripheral element in the larger struggle between Stalin and Tomsky, Rykov, and Bukharin over the peasants and industrialization.

Fitzpatrick believes that Stalin used the cultural revolution as an added weapon to attack and discredit his opponents, and Bukharin certainly was the chief victim. However, it is difficult to extend the left/right political continuum in politics to culture. For example, Trotsky was a political leftist but a cultural rightist, but Bukharin supported *proletkult* (i.e., a leftist position) in the early 1920s but switched to the right after Lenin's death. Bukharin was also the architect of the 1925 policy on art which acknowledged ultimate proletarian hegemony—though by the late 1920s Bukharin was both a political and cultural rightist.

Cultural revolution was in large measure pushed from below over tensions between proletarian and bourgeois groups. In Fitzpatrick's view, NEP did create a bourgeois intelligentsia with special privileges, and as the working class base of mass organizations expanded, resentment developed between young aggressive Communists and the established bourgeois intellectuals. The case of RAPP was interesting because it reflected cultural revolution within a profession where class war was conducted by and on behalf of groups which only claimed to be proletarian and in fact consisted of Communists from white collar or intelligentsia backgrounds. By 1928 RAPP had taken the lead in uncovering the rightist deviation in culture and had achieved power in the realm of literature by its own efforts. RAPP never received formal Party endorsement, and, as Fitzpatrick writes, "This dictatorship, supposedly in the name of the proletarian Party, was in fact not under effective Central Committee control."[9]

In the aftermath of the cultural revolution Fitzpatrick suggests that it was the aggressive Communist intellectuals (those in RAPP, for example) who suffered and became victims. In her view, the general assumption that militant Communists had the support of Stalin is not particularly valid; Stalin's support of the cultural revolution was cautious.[10]

Paradoxically, the old intelligentsia came out of the episode in better shape despite some very harsh treatment. In the 1932–36 period the policies of cultural revolution were essentially reversed, and the old intelligentsia received compensation in the form of material and status improvement.

But there were more positive gains. As part of a general process of social differentiation in the thirties, the privileges of the intelligentsia relative to society as a whole greatly increased. The leaders of the cultural intelligentsia became part of the highest Soviet elite. The "cultural achievements" of the Soviet Union . . . were acclaimed and rewarded by the regime. A genuine poll of intelligentsia opinion taken, say, in 1934, would surely have recorded increased satisfaction with the regime (not only in comparison with 1929, but also with 1924) and expectations of further improvement to come.[11]

However, the group which benefited most were the proletarians who were promoted into jobs and higher education—*vydvizhenie,* the movement for proletarian advancement.[12] The significance of the period of class war cultural revolution, according to Fitzpatrick, may be the fact that the "Brezhnev" generation received the biggest push in this era. This interpretation may hold the key to the later "Stalin revolution" and the new Soviet elite who came to power in the 1960s.

This was the period in which the social and generational tensions of NEP came to a climax in an onslaught (which the leadership only partly controlled) on privilege and established authority. But these were also the first and formative years of the Stalin era. We are accustomed to the idea that the First Five-Year Plan laid the foundations for Stalinist industrialization, just as collectivization laid the foundations for Stalinist agriculture. It should surely be recognized that cultural revolution was an equally important part of what has been called the "Stalin revolution." The substance behind the rhetoric of class war was large-scale upward mobility of industrial workers and working-class Party members into higher education and administrative managerial jobs. Cultural revolution was the vehicle for training the future Communist elite and creating the new Soviet intelligentsia.[13]

The cultural revolution approach to this period has a very direct impact on the issue of RAPP's dissolution and the subsequent developments of socialist realism and the Writers' Union. In this context, socialist realism must be seen as a liberalizing tendency which was part of a larger and more general plan to gain cooperation from the intelligentsia and the skilled "specialists." Primarily, socialist realism was an organizing tool and not an aesthetic—i.e., not a clear, cogent, and comprehensive guide to literary activities.

If, as Fitzpatrick suggests, the rise in the status of bourgeois specialists after 1931 was not temporary or decorative, then the turn to the Writers' Union was a genuine effort at reconciliation. There was censorship and bureaucratic Party control, to be sure, but cultural institutions like the Writers' Union were not designed to be Communist. As Fitzpatrick explains:

When the period of "proletarian hegemony" ended in 1932 with the dissolution of RAPP, a decision was made to organize an all-inclusive Union of Soviet Writers in which literary factions would be dissolved and "bourgeois" non-Communists admitted on equal terms with the Communists. Even the bourgeois avant-gardists, whose reputations as troublemakers almost rivaled that of the proletarians, were admitted and for a few years not attacked. The formula of "socialist realism" which the Union adopted was not originally conceived as a "party line," any more than the Union was conceived as an instrument of total control over literature. Both were initially intended to cancel out the old RAPP line of proletarian and Communist exclusiveness and make room for literary diversity—their disciplinary uses came later, with the mounting political tension of 1935–36.[14]

From this perspective, the period of 1931 to 1934 may be viewed as one in which the cultural intelligentsia was permitted broad diversity. Party membership was not required, and in many instances leadership in cultural areas was turned over to cultural figures who were non-Party. There is a certain political openness in this period that does not conform to the traditional argument of attempts by the Party to inculcate Communist values into cultural activities. The choice of shifting away from proletarian culture and halting the cultural revolution seems to have opened the way for a period of accommodation and compromise.[15]

There is direct evidence to support the contention of liberalization. It is true that a plan for literature was devised, but also that it was not devised by Stalin as a devious ploy for dictatorial control over literature. The guidelines on literature were established not as a separate category but as part of a general Party effort to create a working relationship with fellow travelers.

On April 23, 1932, RAPP was dissolved. The order was short and direct, concentrating on the need for organization changes:

The Central Committee ascertains that, as a result of the considerable successes of socialist construction, literature and art have, in the past few years, exhibited a considerable growth, both in quality and quantity.

Some years ago, when literature was still under the strong influence of certain alien elements, which flourished particularly in the first years of NEP, and when the ranks of proletarian literature were still comparatively feeble, the Party helped, by every means in its power, in the creation of special proletarian organizations in the spheres of literature and art, with a view to strengthening the position of proletarian writers and art workers.

Now that the cadres of proletarian literature have had time to grow, and new writers have come forward from factories, mills, and collective farms, the framework of the existing literary organizations (VOAPP, RAPP, RAPM, etc.) has become too narrow and holds back the serious growth of literary creation. This situation creates the danger that these organizations may be transformed from a means for the greater mobilization of Soviet writers and artists around the tasks of socialist construction into a means for the cultivation of group insulation, for isolation from the political tasks of the day, and from those significant groups of writers and artists who now sympathize with the aims of socialist construction.

Hence the necessity for an appropriate reorganization of the literary-artistic associations and for the extension of the basis of their work.

Therefore the Central Committee resolves:

1. To liquidate the Association of Proletarian Writers (VOAPP, RAPP);

2. To unite all writers upholding the platform of the Soviet power and striving to participate in Socialist construction into a single Union of Soviet Writers with a Communist fraction therein;

3. To promote a similar change in the sphere of other forms of art;

4. To entrust the Organizing Bureau with the working out of practical measures for the application of this resolution.[16]

It seems safe to suggest that the resolution can be taken quite literally— i.e., with many intellectuals supporting Party policies RAPP was no longer the correct form under which they should be organized. The resolution criticized RAPP's exclusionary and sectarian approach to non-proletarian writers, an attitude that was no longer acceptable in a period of accommodation with bourgeois specialists. It also called for unity of all writers in a broad-based organization that included Party fractions. The practical basis for unity within the Writers' Union was, as the Party stated, relatively liberal and unconfining: sympathy for the building of socialism.

Further evidence for this interpretation of the dissolution order appears in a *Pravda* editorial of May 9, 1932, "Na uroven' novykh zadach"–"(Let Us Raise Ourselves) to the Level of New Tasks:"

The decisive successes of socialist construction in the last few years have occasioned a decisive transition of the overwhelming majority of the old technical intelligentsia to the side of the Soviet power, a clear and consistent transition to this position of the greatest scholars of the land, who are giving their great knowledge to the cause of socialism, as shown in part by the fact that the All-Union Academy of Sciences has turned in the direction of working on the contemporary tasks of socialist construction.

In the field of literature this change has been evidenced by the active participation of the broad cadres of writers in socialist construction, and has found its expression in their artistic production (Leonov, Tikhonov, Shaginian, Malyshkin, and others).

. . . .

The organizational structure of the literary and artistic organizations does not answer to the new conditions and new tasks of Soviet literature, especially since elements of clannishness, and administrative methods, in spite of directives from the Party itself, have not been overcome. . . .

Among the most glaring mistakes of a literary character is the insistence on individual psychology. On the basis of this was evolved the idealistic theory of the living man, more fully formulated in the thesis: "The world is man." This conclusion was closely bound up with the following methodological formulation: "The analysis of individual psychology" (Averbakh, *O zadachakh proletarskoi literatury*). . . .

Gross political errors were also made with relation to the fellow-travelers. On the pages of *On Literary Guard* there was cultivated a clearly leftist slogan: "Not fellow-traveler, but ally or enemy!". . .

Such an approach to the task of remaking and reeducating the fellow-travelers radically contradicts the line of the Party. . . .[17]

The editorial is a summary of the Party resolution, a brief critique of RAPP, and an analysis of the significance of the reorganization. It tends to reflect Stalin's ideas about shifts in the old intelligentsia which were elaborated in his 1931 speech "New Conditions, New Tasks." This is the speech in which Stalin suggests that the old policy (circa 1929) of "smashing the active wreckers, separating the neutrals, and enlisting those who are loyal" is no longer necessary and apt because too many of the formerly hostile intelligentsia have "turned to the side of the Soviet government." The new attitude is to enlist and encourage them.[18] The editorial is quite specific in its criticism of RAPP's failure to alter its approach to fellow travelers in light of the new Party line.

The evidence also shows that the efforts at reconciliation were of relatively long duration, lasting from April 1932 until summer 1934. The chronology of events shows commitment to engage fellow travelers as active participants in the creation of the new writers' organization: The First Plenum of the Organizing Committee gathered in October-November 1932 and worked through the next two years, leading to the publishing of proposed by-laws in May 1934; the First Congress of the Writers' Union met in August, 1934. The delays apparent in this chronology indicate not rapid "Stalinization" and regimentation but deliberate and active work to seek support for the new organization and policy.

As stipulated in the April resolution, the responsibility for creating a single Writers' Union was given to a special committee. It was headed by Ivan Gronsky, the editor of *Izvestiya*, with Valery Kirpotin, literary critic and member of the Communist Academy, appointed as secretary. Gorky was the honorary chairman and was given Party authorization to lead in developing the Writers' Union and improving the level of literary production. Other Party representatives included Pavel Yudin, philosopher, and later editor of *Literatury Kritik*, and Lev Subotsky, secretary of the Literary Organization of the Red Army and Navy. Though the Organizing Committee was led by Gronsky and Kirpotin, it was composed initially of twenty-four members, of whom nine were fellow travelers and nine were former members of RAPP—not associated with the Averbakh clique, though later Averbakh was asked to participate.[19]

It is undeniable that Gronsky, Kirpotin, and Subotsky were developing a specific retrospective criticism of RAPP and advocating a new organization with a new slogan. But if the process of "subverting" literature to Party domination was decided and the slogan and method determined, why create an environment for open discussion and debate lasting almost two years (the Second Plenum met in February 1933 and the Third in May 1934)? In reality, the organizing meetings provided opportunities for discussion among competing groups.

The stenographic record of the First Plenum of the Organizing Committee shows the nature of this discussion and debate. It indicates that the meeting was not a contrived setting in which Party spokesmen enunciated the guidelines of socialist realism, setting boundaries for debate. The stenographic record does show that Gronsky, Kirpotin, and Subotsky gave the major addresses, but their comments went beyond simply defining socialist realism. There was discussion and criticism of RAPP. They named many writers whose works reflected their shift to the support of socialist construction necessitating increased material support by the state for writers. Interestingly, the record of the plenum also reveals that fellow travelers, those who had previously been under attack, used the meeting to articulate much of their resentment at RAPP's policies.[20]

The direct results of the debate and discussion during the two years of the Organizing Committee's work are best seen in the promulgation of the constitution of the Writers' Union. While it may be argued that the definition of socialist realism which emerged from the Third Plenum was a sharply proscriptive guide to literary work, it should be noted that the definition appeared finally as part of the constitution in the section on rules:

Socialist realism, being the basic method of Soviet imaginative literature and literary criticism, demands from the artist a truthful, historically concrete depiction of reality in its revolutionary development. At the same time this truthfulness and historical concreteness of the artistic depiction of reality must be combined with the task of ideological molding and education of the working people in the spirit of socialism.[21]

The rules of the Union of Soviet Writers also offer some softening elaboration of the definition: "Socialist realism guarantees to artistic production the exclusive possibility of the manifestation of creative initiative of the choice of various forms, styles, and genres. . . ."[22] This may be little more than window dressing, given the repression later in the decade, but it certainly suggests something less than dogmatism of a single style.

In the second section of the rules the political demands are explained. Here the writer is asked through his creative work to support socialist construction. The third and fourth sections outline membership regulations and governing bodies, respectively. The fifth section, which delineates the legal and material rights given by the state, reads in part:

2. The Directorate of the Union of Soviet Writers has the right to organize a series of auxiliary organizations operating under their own independent constitutions or by resolution of the Directorate. These organizations shall have the goal of helping writers culturally and materially. Such organizations are writers' homes, clubs, rest homes, museums, libraries, reading rooms, bookstores, courses, exhibitions, contests, publishing houses, journals, etc.[23]

It is certainly possible to suggest that a single Writers' Union may be seen as an easy organization to control; it must also be acknowledged that the rules published and accepted by the congress were designed to unite writers into a *professional* union providing some institutional guarantees of support and elevation in status and pay.

Finally, there are three pieces of indirect evidence which tend to support the thesis that the development of socialist realism reflected an organizational restructuring in line with a more liberal policy toward intellectuals and technical specialists. First, Stalin's report to the Seventeenth Party Congress in January 1934 emphasized organizational restructuring in all aspects of Soviet life. Devoted mainly to the advances made under the First Five-Year Plan, the report summarizes the accomplishments in building socialism but also points ahead to new goals and directions. In the third section of the report on Party issues, Stalin concentrates on the necessary organizational changes required to fulfill the guidelines for consolidating the socialist construction during the Second Five-Year Plan as outlined by the Seventeenth Party Conference (January-February 1932)—the conference at which the theme of building a "socialist society" was announced.[24]

Second, the general problem of organizational restructuring is taken up in a speech delivered at the Seventeenth Congress by L. M. Kaganovich, a member of the Politburo and a supporter of Stalin. The lengthy speech is primarily concerned with organizational questions in the spheres of agriculture and industry, not literature and culture. Kaganovich argues that a wide variety of organizational changes will be needed, with the Central Committee leading the way in a number of areas. But Kaganovich sees the responsibility for fulfillment of the general Party line devolving on individual members.

In part of his conclusion he urges members to "multiply the forces of the Bolsheviks by winning the broad masses to our side—primarily the non-Party activists, the workers, office employees, the specialists. ..."[25] This speech seemed primarily designed to announce that the Central Committee was interested mainly in thoroughgoing organizational reform. Interestingly, at the end of his speech he makes a brief aside about literary reorganization:

I will quote an example from a sphere that would seem to be least operative; I refer to the sphere of literature. ... I have in mind the case of RAPP. As you know a group of Communist writers, utilizing the organizational instrument of the RAPP, exercised their Communist influence on the literary front in a wrong way, and instead of enlisting broad cadres of writers and uniting them around the RAPP, this group of comrades hindered the development of creative literary forces. In this case the Central Committee came up against the wrong political line of a number of Communist writers on the literary front who had an organizational apparatus ... at their disposal.

Of course, a long resolution could have been drawn up enumerating the tasks of the Communist in the field of literature and the RAPP could have been instructed to change its line. But this would have only remained a pious wish. Comrade Stalin raised the question in a different way. He said: the situation must be changed organizationally. And then the question of dissolving RAPP and of forming a single Writers' Union was raised. After this organizational solution of the problem, the writing forces in the country developed and the situation . . . is improving. Thus the solution of an organizational problem secured the correct carrying out of the Party line in the field of literature.[26]

The example of RAPP in his speech is but one of several arguing for the need to increase supervision and control of Party decisions—supervision in the constructive sense of improvement, not punishment. RAPP was cited as an example to illustrate Central Committee operations. Kaganovich seemed to have intended it as an explanation of how the Central Committee worked to help Party members carry out organizational restructuring. While it is possible to argue that increased interest on the part of the Central Committee meant increasing politicization, it is not equivalent to dictatorship from above.

The third bit of indirect evidence involves the speeches of Andrey Zhdanov, Nikolai Bukharin, and Karl Radek at the First Writers' Congress. It is usually argued that Zhdanov's speech marks the beginning of direct Stalinist intervention in literary life. Zhdanov is presented as a Stalinist who concentrated exclusively on the ideological aspects of literature. This is in contrast to Bukharin's liberal comments.[27] While it is no doubt true that Bukharin and Radek were active at the First Congress with the forbearance of the Party, it does seem odd that if Stalinization of literature was well advanced by 1934 there would be a need to include these men on the platform. Again, the proposition (given their elimination later in the decade) that they may have been used as calling cards for the fellow travelers is one possible explanation. The illusion of liberalization may have been the plan, but it seems equally feasible that the creation of the Writers' Union was an attempt, at least in 1934, to establish an umbrella organization in line with a general Party program of rapprochement.

Interestingly, Aleksey Stetsky's (manager of the Culture and Leninist Propaganda Section of the Central Committee) speech is rarely cited in the Western non-Marxist analyses. He characterizes the congress as ". . . marked by free, creative discussion of all literary problems. It is not passing any resolutions on literary questions that are binding on all writers." And he carefully states that "socialist realism is not some set of tools that are handed out to the writer for him to make a work of art."[28]

The fairest assessment of the work of the Organizational Committee in its plenums leading to the First Congress is that it created a professional organization for writers based on the organizational directive issued in the April 1932 resolution. There was widespread and optimistic support for the new union, as evidenced by the speeches and attendance at the Congress. The rules published and accepted by the delegates were designed primarily to unite writers into one union in which there was a Communist fraction; the idea first articulated in 1932 was executed in 1934.

The totalitarian model based on the hypothesis of a "Stalinist dictatorship" with its conscious plan to subvert literature is not supported by evidence. Such an approach tends to read back out of context the Zhdanov period of 1946–53 and the repression of the purges beginning in 1936. It requires a view of the thirties as an era dominated by political repression and executions. The RAPP leadership came under especially harsh attack, with many of its leaders disappearing and many more discredited. It is a view that suggests that the purges of the mid-thirties were planned as early as 1932, and therefore the creation of socialist realism and the Writers' Union were designed at the outset to perform the functions of censorship, control, and punishment.

It is pointless, of course, to consider socialist realism and the Writers' Union outside of the Communist political context. This was not an invitation for open and unfettered debate. The fellow travelers, smarting from the attacks and repression of RAPP, were particularly sensitive to the political aspects of the reorganization. Socialist realism and the Writers' Union were used as organizing tools. But as we have seen, the 1932–34 period was marked by liberalization, an easing of tensions, in which the Party did not lay down an aesthetic line. The proletarian and class war line was pervasive under RAPP, but it was not the official line. In fact, there was no official Party line on literature even as late as 1934.

With internal literary affairs of the Soviet Union in flux, on what basis can it be suggested that the Soviet Union was providing direct and conscious guidance to the CPUSA on cultural matters? This question will be considered in the next chapter as we review the American response to events in the Soviet Union. Fundamentally, the proletarian phase which was deemphasized in the Soviet Union beginning in 1932 continued in America well beyond the 1935 opening of the united front.

CHAPTER 3

SOVIET SOCIALIST REALISM AND THE CPUSA
The View From America

The shift by the CPSU in its approach to writers in the period from the dissolution of RAPP and the formation of the Writers' Union was a sharp and significant political and organizational change. However, American Communists, including both the literary doyens (Mike Gold, Joshua Kunitz, and Joseph Freeman), and political leaders specializing in cultural matters (A. B. Magil, Alexander Trachtenberg, and V. J. Jerome) never really provided a serious analysis of the post-1932 changes in Soviet literary affairs. The absence of interpretation by American Communists exposes one part of the real separation between Party politics and culture in the 1930s; such separation is characteristic of the entire decade, though it becomes more distinct during the popular front.

It also reflects, ironically (given the traditional literature), an unexpectedly low level of Soviet influence on American literary affairs. Americans did not follow the Soviet lead for broadening relations with sympathetic supporters until after 1935 and the creation of the united front line.

Specifically, direct discussion of the Congress of Soviet Writers, of the term "socialist realism," and of the dissolution of RAPP was quite limited in America. Moissaye J. Olgin, who attended the Soviet congress, reported the event and summarized the speeches in two articles for the *New Masses*.[1] Later his observations of the congress were recast for his speech at the First American Writers' Congress in April 1935. Presented in somewhat pep-rally terms, the glorification of the Soviet congress was an understandable mixture of puff for Soviet culture and restatements of slogans.

In Olgin's version, the Soviet congress was at once evidence of the "colossal growth" of Soviet culture, of the reconciliation between writers

40

and the Party, of the conversion of writers to socialism, of the success of the Party line on proletarian revolution, of writers' importance as "engineers of the human soul," and of the worldwide development of revolutionary literature. As inspiration for the American congress perhaps this speech was of some value, but it was not, as we have seen, an accurate analysis of the changes within the Soviet Union.[2]

At least one observer thought the Soviet Writers' Congress and the term "socialist realism" should be understood analytically. As part of the preliminary discussions about the American Writers' Congress, Robert Gessner suggested that an important task for the congress was to learn to interpret the value of the Soviet experience. He asked the important question: "How can the stirring challenge and vision of socialist realism be applied to American revolutionary writers?"

His hope was that the congress would answer the question. It was not answered at the congress or by the Party.[3] There was one direct effort to define the term "socialist realism." It was an essay written by Edwin Seaver in 1935 for the *New Masses*. But it too was primarily summation and extracts from the main speeches at the Soviet Writers' Congress.[4]

Though the emergence of a Soviet Writers' Union was reported and the slogan of socialist realism was cited, the scant evidence of direct and thoughtful analysis suggests a rather lax connection to Soviet literary and Party affairs. It also suggests a rather unsophisticated view of the strategy of the CPSU to attract writers and intellectuals in the early 1930s.[5]

The difficulty of making a direct connection to Soviet literary life is often finessed by arguing that Soviet directives were passed through the International Union of Revolutionary Writers (IURW)—the literary arm of the Comintern dominated completely by RAPP. Of special significance was the Second International Conference of Revolutionary and Proletarian Writers (1930), known as the Kharkov Conference. It is clear that a series of resolutions adopted at the Kharkov Conference were the basis for the proletarian literary movement emphasized by the *New Masses* and the John Reed Clubs in the early thirties. But that the Kharkov resolutions were orders from Moscow is not supported by the evidence.

The proletarian Kharkov resolutions were the dominant guidelines for American Communists from 1930 to 1935, including the first American Writers' Congress. The important progression of events in the Soviet Union climaxing in the August 1934 Writers' Congress was never detailed or explored by American Communists. In reference to the Soviet Union, the CPUSA was tied to an obviously outmoded literary policy. The work of American Communists in culture during the first half of the decade was tied organizationally, theoretically, and artistically to the Kharkov

Conference—which of course was controlled by the Soviet Union. But the Soviet delegation was led by RAPP, a group soon to be displaced.

The work of the *New Masses* and the John Reed Clubs to advance proletarian culture had as its foundation two resolutions promulgated at the Kharkov Conference. One was the general resolution "On Political and Creative Questions of International Proletarian and Revolutionary Literature." Its thesis was ". . . only the triumph of the Socialist Revolution can create the necessary conditions for the complete development of proletarian culture. But even in the period immediately preceding the social revolution, namely imperialism, the proletariat is creating a culture of its own which will serve its revolutionary purposes."[6] RAPP's imprint is most clearly seen in the section of the resolution on artistic method where proletarian literature is tagged as ". . . nothing more than a weapon in the class struggle." And proletarian culture is further defined:

. . . This means that every proletarian artist must be a dialectical materialist. The creative method of proletarian literature is the method of dialectical materialism. For ours is the art of a class engaged in revolutionary re-making of the world, a class whose outlook is free of petty bourgeois limitations and of bourgeois misrepresentation of reality, a class which rends all veils, and destroys all false conceptions of reality in order to gain an objective knowledge of reality, and on the basis of this to achieve a revolutionary transformation of that reality.[7]

The general resolution also makes passing reference to the responsibilities of the IURW and the individual parties. Basically, the message conveyed was to use proletarian literature as an ideological weapon. However, the resolution fails to assign specific duties to the Party except to state that as the proletarian movement grows the Party's role will expand. The IURW was given the duty of raising the theoretical level of Marxism-Leninism as it applies to art, though there is little evidence of this activity after 1932—because it was a RAPP organization.[8]

The American delegation (Fred Ellis, Michael Gold, William Gropper, Joshua Kunitz, A. B. Magil, and Harry Allan Potamkin) returned to America with a ten-point resolution outlining a program of activity for building a "proletarian-revolutionary cultural movement" in the U.S. The primary goal was to expand the activities of the John Reed Clubs and the *New Masses* by (1) "extending the proletarian base of our movement by drawing in new proletarian elements," and (2) "winning over of radicalized intellectuals."[9] It is worth noting the efforts directed at fulfilling the specific goals:

1. The National Committee for the Defense of Political Prisoners (chaired by Theodore Dreiser) was organized in the spring of 1931 to

involve writers and intellectuals directly in political campaigns—i.e., Scottsboro, Tom Mooney, the coal strikes (such as in Harlan, Kentucky).[10]

2. The Workers Cultural Federation was formed to extend cultural activities beyond intellectuals to workers. This attempt at a national federation was not successful, though it was an interesting experiment trying to link writers to factory, cultural, language, and sports groups. Also, the Revolutionary Writers Federation, a section of the WCF, initiated in 1932 a monthly literary service of poems, short stories, and plays edited by Keene Wallis of the New York JRC.[11]

3. The central proposition of a manifesto prepared by the JRC of New York for presentation to the National Organizing Conference held in Chicago in May 1932 was a call for writers and artists to join the JRC on the basis of the Kharkov program.[12]

4. The shift of the *New Masses* to a weekly beginning in January 1934 was also part of the attempt to implement Kharkov goals. The new weekly was to concentrate more on political analysis at the expense of the older bohemian radicalism.[13]

5. The creation of the Professional Groups for Foster/Ford (PGFF) to support the Communist candidates in the 1932 general election was part of the program begun at the Kharkov Conference.[14]

Some further insight into the relationship between the Soviet Union and the CPUSA is provided by a stinging debate sparked by the Trotsky supporter Max Eastman, who attacked the Kharkov Conference, claiming it put "artists in uniform." Of interest in the debate between Eastman and the Party spokesmen is both the refutation of Eastman's charges and their rather obvious ignorance of the cultural changes in the Soviet Union during this crucial period.

Eastman attacked the Kharkov Conference as the beginnings of American acceptance of Soviet orders on the literary front.[15] The conference provided an easy target because there was the convenient ten-point program and the gradual efforts to implement it (noted above). Eastman used these facts as evidence of subservience to Moscow.[16]

The response to Eastman's charges was swift. In the first of two *New Masses* articles, Joshua Kunitz stated that a rigid formula was not imposed on writers at the conference and then later annulled. He denied any attempt at enforcement either at Kharkov or after RAPP's demise. Responding to Eastman's claim that RAPP's method of dialectical materialism was imposed at this conference and then replaced by socialist realism, Kunitz writes: ". . . he seeks to show that a rigid formula for creative work was imposed . . . second, that this superimposed formula was later annulled, and another substituted in its place, also from the top and finally . . . each in turn rammed down the throats of the John Reed Club and the *New Masses*, turned members of those organizations into artists in uniform."[17]

In his second essay Kunitz concentrated on refuting Eastman's charge that cultural life in the Soviet Union was now inferior and that the arts had been humiliated under Stalinist slogans. For Kunitz, "The truth is, there is no other country in the contemporary world where the arts are so vital, so earnest, where the creative artist, even the beginner, enjoys such prestige and economic security as in the Soviet Union."[18] As for the controversial need to create slogans, Kunitz accepted it somewhat uncritically:

> Just as untrue as Mr. Eastman's assertions about the regimentation of all art in the Soviet Union under the dialectical materialist banner are his assertions that dialectical materialism has been summarily dethroned and "Socialist realism" and "red romanticism" put in its stead. Such a formulation is of course nonsensical, for Socialist realism is nothing but the literary equivalent of dialectical materialism. There is no contradiction, and there has been no dethroning. A writer permeated with the dialectical materialist philosophy . . . is bound to be a socialist realist. . . .[19]

Here is an example of a leading American Communist authority on Russian literature who obviously failed to understand the organizational and political changes in Soviet literary life, or rather actually explained them in terms of labels and slogans. In both his articles there is the suggestion that RAPP was simply too narrow —i.e., with few writers actually belonging as members.

When he reviews Eastman's book eight months later, Kunitz still does not discuss reorganization but once again concentrates on slogans:

> . . . the slogans about Proletarian Art, the Magnitostroy of Literature, the Living Man, Art as a Weapon, Dialectical Materialist Art, Socialist Realism, Socialist Romanticism, etc., are not expressions of a Stalin pulling strings, but a manifestation of tumultuous forces released by the revolution and driven from the depths to the surface of life. They are understandable, inevitable, and useful. And Eastman's sneers (how he does manage to befoul everything he touches!) simply prove that in his airiness he is not at all attuned to the new forces and their riotous tempo.[20]

Kunitz argues that Eastman misunderstood Soviet literature because of his refusal to accept slogans. In essence, Kunitz's disagreement with Eastman tends to become an argument over the correct interpretation of slogans as they apply to literature.

In another attack on Eastman's book by a Party writer, there is further evidence of the disinterest in or ignorance of organizational changes in the Soviet Union. Leon Dennen flatly rejects Eastman's "artist in uniform" label. Part of Dennen's refutation is a brief synopsis of Russian literary affairs viewing RAPP's ascendancy on the basis of its membership's energy and zeal as Communists. Dennen believes that RAPP's slogan "dialectical materialism" was a positive contribution since it was part of the struggle to give writers a revolutionary outlook. According to Dennen, RAPP was dissolved because it did not appeal to the increasing numbers of older writers who were now accepting the socialist revolution.[21]

Beyond the Eastman controversy, there is one other event that affects this question of American subordination to the Soviet Union. Many observers suggest that the decision by American Communists to call a writers' congress was a direct imitation of the Soviet experience. The argument is generally presented in the following way. In late September 1934, at the national meeting of the JRC, Alexander Trachtenberg, representing the Central Committee of the CPUSA, suggested the organizing of a writers' congress. He made this suggestion because it mirrored directly the recently concluded Soviet congress. Not only are these events interpreted as orders from Moscow but they are usually seen as a directive from the CC imposed without discussion upon a somewhat unwilling JRC membership.[22]

The evidence does not easily support such a view. Though it is clear that the Party, through Trachtenberg, initiated the congress and through Party members organized it, there is no evidence to suggest that it was imposed on the JRC.[23] In calling for such a congress of writers, Trachtenberg noted that creative literature had an important function in fighting capitalism, and that too often the proletarian movement underestimated the radicalism of American writers. He asked that the newly elected National Committee of the JRC be responsible for preparing the congress on an anti-fascist and broad-based platform to be held within eight weeks. The idea was apparently accepted enthusiastically, and the National Committee was instructed to proceed.

A review of the documents shows that Trachtenberg was suggesting that cultural activities should be less sectarian, and that sympathetic writers should not be confronted with either joining the Party or being perceived as outcasts. He drew no analogy to the Soviet experience. Furthermore, the reports of the National Conference, though critical of the narrowness of the JRC, made no effort to connect American and Soviet experiences.

The following conclusions about the ties between the Soviet Union and the CPUSA can be made safely. First, the 1935 American Writers' Congress was organized on the basic principles of the Kharkov Conference of 1930, not on the model of the 1934 Soviet Writers' Union:

The program for the League of American Writers would be evolved at the Congress, basing itself on the following: fight against imperialist war and fascism; defend the Soviet Union against capitalist aggression; for the development and strengthening of the revolutionary labor movement; against white chauvinism (against all forms of Negro discrimination or persecution) and against the persecution of minority groups and of the foreign born; solidarity with colonial people in their struggles; against the influence of bourgeois ideas in American liberalism; against the imprisonment of revolutionary writers and artists, as well as other class-war prisoners throughout the world.[24]

The call to the First American Writers' Congress sounded the same chords as the 1930 Kharkov resolutions: (1) What is the best way to take "effective political action against war and fascism?" and (2) How to present in writers' work the "fresh understanding of the American scene that has come from the enrollment in the revolutionary cause?" It was a reaffirmation of the Kharkov principles. The calling of the congress and the establishment of the League of American Writers did not yet mark a new position. The shift came later, after the adoption of the united front policies of the Seventh Comintern Congress.[25] And it required almost two years to adjust cultural activities in America to this change—represented by the Second American Writers' Congress in the spring of 1937.

The second and third conclusions about Soviet and American connections are rather straightforward. The American Communists involved with literature had a very incomplete understanding of the reorganization of the 1932-34 period. Beyond sensing the turn of many writers toward the acceptance of Soviet socialism (a move to the left which they witnessed in America as well) and the emergence of a new slogan to reflect that change, there was no evaluation of the political basis for the Soviet changes. And finally, there was no concerted effort to disband quickly the JRC or dismantle the proletarian magazines.[26]

The fact is that the American CP adhered tenaciously to the 1930 program. Its approach to literature cannot be explained as one that followed the Soviet lead. Apparently, the American position was little if at all influenced by the creation of the Soviet Writers' Union. As we shall see, it was the liberalizing trend of the post-1935 period that eased relations between the Party and leftist intellectuals. The lead suggested by the Soviet congress for broadening relations with sympathetic supporters was not followed in the U.S. until after the establishment of the popular front. Not until the Second Writers' Congress in 1937 was there a move to structure a truly broad-based association of writers. Of course, in the Soviet Union the Party held state power and thus could act with a speed and authority far beyond anything possible for the CPUSA. But the persistence of the Kharkov line does reveal how little emphasis was placed on relations with intellectuals and on literary problems.

The Kharkov program was adopted by Party members active in the cultural area, but there is no evidence to suggest that it was discussed thoroughly throughout the Party. In the Soviet Union, as I see it, there was a clear and logical development of a new Party program. In America there was a proletarian emphasis without a very clear attachment to the Party programs. It seems clear that there was no decision to demolish quickly the JRC and end proletarian literature as part of the plan to organize a writers' congress. The shift in emphasis is tied far more directly to the later event of the united front as developed at the Seventh Comintern Congress in August 1935.

PART 2

THE CPUSA AND CULTURE
IN THE 1930s

CHAPTER 4

AMERICAN INTELLECTUALS
AND THE PARTY

The twenty-fifth anniversary issue of the *New Masses* (December 15, 1936) illustrates the cultural popular front at its unified and tranquil best. Appearing in that issue were the leading Party spokesmen on culture—Joseph Freeman, Mike Gold, Granville Hicks, and Isidor Schneider—and with them a variety of contributors both in and out of the Party: Earl Browder, John Strachey, Rex Stout, Agnes Smedley, John Dos Passos, George Seldes, Scott Nearing, Upton Sinclair, Sherwood Anderson, Theodore Dreiser, Vincent Sheean, Albert Halper, John Howard Lawson, Albert Maltz, Maxwell Bodenheim, Alfred Kreymborg, Genevieve Taggard, Richard Wright, Sarah Cleghorn, Louis Untermeyer, Langston Hughes, William Gropper, and others.[1]

But by 1939, after the defeat of Loyalist Spain and the announcement of the Hitler-Stalin pact, Ralph Bates, the British novelist and weary Spanish War veteran (employing the well-worn metaphor of the Red express), said it best, "I am getting off the train. . ."[2] And, of course, many other fellow traveling and Party literary heavyweights disembarked with him: Granville Hicks, Malcolm Cowley, Vincent Sheean, Archibald MacLeish, Lewis Mumford, Paul de Kruif, Matthew Josephson, Harold Laski, John Strachey, and Victor Gollancz, to name but a few of the well-known international figures.[3]

They joined a group which had stepped off somewhat earlier (mainly at the Moscow trials) and had created in 1936 an American Committee for the Defense of Leon Trotsky, which became the subsequent Committee for Cultural Freedom and thus for organized anti-Communism by leftist intellectuals.[4]

The shattering of the popular front has become a central theme in the cultural histories of Communism and intellectuals during the 1930s. The moments of apostasy and the disavowal of the Party and its politics have been used for both moral and political redemption by the disaffected intellectuals—described most often in memoir literature.

Because this group was so vocal and visible, their experiences with the Party have been overemphasized and have led to two serious distortions. First, focusing so intensely and melodramatically on these intellectuals tempts one to consider the popular front as primarily a cultural phenomenon.[5] This obscures the political basis of the popular front strategy and fails to consider the most significant aspect, which was, of course, trade union work. Second, scrutinizing the cultural popular front through the disillusioning events of Spain, the trials, and the pact exaggerates the intellectuals' significance in the life and program of the Party.[6]

To trace the paths of the intellectuals as they withdrew support from the Party and became disenchanted with politics tacitly imposes on these events an interpretation which demonstrates: first, the return to sanity of the intellectuals, and second, the deception and duplicity of Communist leadership and program. The illusion is that the Party had a carefully and decisively planned program for culture and intellectuals that failed. But if the emphasis is reversed and the Party documents are analyzed without a prior assumption, a rather opposite view emerges: the Party never developed a coherent plan for intellectuals, and never really gave much consideration to the question of proper relations with this group.

In the pre-1935 proletarian phase the Party's basic approach was to build alliances with intellectuals who were willing to break with the bourgeoisie and support the workers. The primary goal was to cultivate writers from the proletariat, but a secondary goal was to cultivate fellow travelers who were sympathetic to the idea of the victory of proletariat. However, the middle class writers had to be screened very carefully to separate the "genuinely" revolutionary from those considered renegades (e. g., Max Eastman) and "social fascists" (V. F. Calverton).

For example, when Sidney Hook declared himself an unaffiliated Marxist after having served as a chairman of several campaign functions for the William Z. Foster and James W. Ford ticket in 1932, he was soundly attacked for his revisionism. The skepticism of the Party toward the politically unstable middle class intellectuals was clear:

The identification of the intellectuals with the revolutionary movement is dependent, however, on their complete rift with bourgeois ideology and liberalism. . . . The relationship of the intellectuals as a group with the working class is essentially an alliance. . . . Only in this alliance will the intellectuals achieve their liberation from their retainership of capitalism, their liberation for working with the proletariat, for helping in the job of revolution.[7]

The most candid and precise explanation of the relationship of the Party to cultural workers in the pre-united front period was Earl Browder's address to the First American Writers' Congress in April 1935, reflecting the previously discussed Kharkov program. He acknowledged that most of the participants at the congress were not affiliated with the Party but were writers who had realized that they must take a position in the battle between capitalists and workers. Browder suggested that, once choosing the workers' side, writers inevitably became involved with the political party of the workers, the CP. His statement is worth quoting at length:

. . . Does the Party claim a leading role in the field of fine literature? If so, upon what basis?

Our Party claims to give political guidance directly to its members, in all fields of work, including the arts. How strong such leadership can be exerted upon non-Party people depends entirely upon the quality of the work of our members. . . .

That means that the first demand of the Party upon its writer-members is that they shall be good writers, constantly better writers, for only so can they really serve the Party. We do not want to take good writers and make bad strike leaders of them.

The Party has such a leading role as its members can win for it by the quality of their work. From this flows the conclusion, that the method of our work in this field cannot be one of Party resolutions giving judgment upon artistic, aesthetic questions. There is no fixed "Party line" by which works of art can be automatically separated into sheep and goats. . . . We can therefore reassure all those who feel there is some truth in the stories about Communists that we want to "control" you, to put you "in uniform." . . .

Second is the question: Does the Communist Party want to "politicalize" the writers of fine literature, by imposing upon them its pre-conceived ideas of subject matter, treatment and form?

We would desire . . . to arouse consciousness among all writers of the political problems of the day, and trace out the relationship of these political problems to the problems of literature. We believe that the overwhelming bulk of fine writing has political significance. We would like to see all writers conscious of this, therefore able to control and direct the political results of their work.

By no means do we think this can be achieved by imposing any preconceived patterns upon the writer. On the contrary, we believe that fine literature must arise directly out of life. . . . The Party wants to help . . . to bring to writers a great new wealth of material. . . .[8]

Browder wanted the support of these writers to help in the struggle for a new society, but not at the expense of the destruction of culture from the past that still had value. He saw the Party's function as providing a connection between the organized writers and organized audience. He assigned three tasks to the writers' group: (1) setting standards; (2) winning new collaborators, both established writers and novices; and (3) attacking the economic problems of writers.

In an interesting aside he noted that the Party had tried to help the *New Masses* precisely because of its potential to aid in fulfilling these tasks. It was especially important, he felt, in its efforts to tie the middle class to the workers:

The *New Masses,* since it was changed from a monthly sixteen months ago, is no longer primarily a cultural organ. It is a *political* weekly with strong cultural interests. . . . While not a party organ, the *New Masses* represents the Communist line. . . . Its new role has not served to discourage cultural publications as such; on the contrary, it is precisely in the last sixteen months that we have witnessed the greatest growth of purely literary publications on the "left." [9]

After the implementation of the united front, work with intellectuals became far easier, since the measure of political commitment was antifascism; in practice, it became support for the labor movement and the mass organizations. The thrust of the Party's work with intellectuals after 1935 was to encourage anti-fascist alliances and to organize professional trade unions. Because the work with intellectuals was undercut by the troubles over the trials, Spain, and ultimately the pact, the Party documents discussing intellectuals tend in large measure to be rebuttals defending the trials and Communist activity in Spain.[10]

The Party's basic laissez faire attitude toward literary intellectuals enunciated by Browder at the First Congress was expanded and recast in popular front terms in his address to the Second Writers' Congress. Held in New York City in June 1937, it took for its themes anti-fascism and the building of a popular front writers' group for professionals. The congress was called by the LAW to consolidate the regional writers' organizations that emerged after the 1935 congress and to encourage unity among writers in their opposition to fascist wars in Spain and Ethiopia. A unifying theme was the argument that an important social function of writers is to help fight against repression and reaction through the defense of democratic cultural traditions and freedoms.[11]

Earl Browder's speech most accurately reflects the united front politics of the Party with regard to intellectuals. The central political struggle, Browder explained, was the fight against reaction, fascism, and war. Writers who do not oppose fascism will only aid the reactionaries, and to aid the reactionaries is to fight against the "people." He restates the Party approach to writers:

We of the Communist Party heartily welcome this great movement of the writers to enter the service of the masses of the people. At your first

Congress we made clear that we do not approach the writers with any ambition to transform them into union organizers, or leaflet distributors. We join wholeheartedly with those who say the task of the writer is to write and to write more and better . . . schemes, blueprints and formal discipline are of less worth in your files than in any other. We Communists are the last to want to regiment the writers; you will work out your own discipline. . . . [12]

In discussing the politics of the united front, he suggests there is no separation between artists and politics, because the fundamental issue is fighting fascism. So the writer has little to fear. He does not ask writers to submit to Party discipline because the Party's goal is unity of all progressive forces. He claims, "Those who in the sacred name of freedom would break our unity in the face of the menace of fascism and war are contributing to the destruction of all freedom." He concludes his address by welcoming all, of no matter what political allegiance: "We are united in our determination to defend culture, to unite culture with the strivings of the people to preserve and extend our democratic heritage. . . ." [13]

How these general principles were converted into a strategy for work with intellectuals is not easy to determine. The only bit of direct evidence is a vague and rhetorical piece written by William Z. Foster in 1938 suggesting that since so many professionals were now joining the Party it was time to begin a serious study of the problem.[14] The difficulty with this piece is that the united front strategy for professionals (Foster's term includes doctors, lawyers, engineers, scientists, teachers, writers, musicians, and actors but excludes white collar office employees) is mixed with rhetoric about the revolutionary potential of the Party, about its vanguard role in the class struggle, about the opportunism of the Socialist Party in dealing with middle class groups, and about the middle class as potential converts to fascism.

Foster believes that if cultivated correctly these professionals can be of great service to "democracy and socialism," carrying the Party's anti-fascist message to the ranks of the white collar middle class ("the strata from which the fascists ordinarily draw heavy forces"). They can help build the democratic front and can be of direct support to the proletariat. And if their political development is high enough, professionals can "do serious theoretical work." [15]

While calling for selective recruiting of professionals and their intensive training in Marxism, Foster reemphasizes that their central purpose is to carry out the united front strategy of working in their respective associations, guilds, and unions—known as the "mass work." It is worth quoting Foster at length:

1. The foundation of the mass work of our Communist professionals

must be a systematic defense of the economic and political interests of the rank-and-file membership of their respective callings . . . .

2. The fight of our professionals must also be linked up with that of the masses generally. Professionals, properly organized, and with a Communist outlook . . . are in a position to lend powerful aid to the masses in the struggle—by speaking and writing, giving financial backing, developing the moral and electoral support, etc. They can become a strong pillar of the democratic front. . . .

3. . . . a vital part of the work of Communist professionals must be to bring the vitally necessary services of their respective professions to the needy masses. Thus our doctors must be the first-line champions of an adequate government health program, our lawyers must fight for free legal aid for the masses, our teachers must still further popularize education, our actors must democratize the theatre, our writers must find ways to bring good literature and effective political writing to the masses, etc., etc.

4. . . . They must take up the intellectual cudgels against the reactionaries on all fronts. Thus our teachers must write new school textbooks and rewrite history from the Marxian viewpoint, our scientists must organize more effectively the battle of materialists against idealists . . . our doctors must introduce new methods into medicine, our lawyers must challenge prevalent musty capitalist legal conceptions and rewrite our legal history, our writers must bring forward class-struggle themes in literature and the theatre.[16]

This program was designed to build organizations where none existed and to link professionals with workers through common struggles. He writes: "Therefore, the various problems and tasks presented by the entry of middle-class professionals into our Party all boil down to the issue of how to make use of the latter to further our central objective of broadening and strengthening the proletarian base and mass leading role of the Communist Party"[17]

The central contradiction is, of course, the existence of both the program for reformist work in the professional organizations and separate revolutionary claims. This contradiction was created when the Party dropped its independent revolutionary Communist line—unnecessarily, in my opinion—to promote the unity of the popular front. The politics of the popular front then becomes union organizing, anti-fascist organization building, and the agitation for the immediate relief of depression ills. The basic tactic tied to the strategy discussed above was the creation and building of *unions*.

The earlier revolutionary and proletarian groups such as the John Reed Clubs, the New Dance League, the Theatre Union, the Film and Foto League were deemphasized or replaced by efforts to create broad-based professional associations or unions. Perhaps the best known of the writers' groups was the League of American Writers. But Communists were also extremely active in the American Newspaper Guild, the Radio Writers Guild, and the Dramatists Guild. When the arts projects developed within the Works Progress Administration, Communists became active in the American Artists' Congress and the American Writers' Union. This latter group worked to unionize the unemployed writers in the Federal Writers' Projects and in Hallie Flanagan's Federal Theatre Project. (Other well-known attempts to organize professionals included the Hollywood Anti-Nazi League, the National Lawyers Guild, the Physicians Forum, and the Teachers Union.)[18]

The most intense review of Party activity in culture during the united front period came from Party spokesmen in response to the desertion of many intellectuals after the signing of the pact. But conspicuously absent from these analyses was a discussion of a specific Party program for intellectuals. There were shrill and petulant ad hominem attacks, disquisitions in support of the democratic front, and complex arguments against participation in an imperialist war.[19] In terms of Communist presence, their central argument is a vague notion of a "guiding hand": (1) Communists revived the democratic tradition of culture in the 1930s by debunking the impotent and reactionary philosophies of the 1920s and by providing opportunities for intellectuals to continue their historical role in the development of Western democratic traditions; (2) the renegades deserted democracy under pressure of reaction fomented by capitalist war and separated themselves from the historic experience of the thirties in which mass struggle for democracy was fused with Communist ideas.

According to Mike Gold, the peripatetic editor/novelist/columnist/ideolog, the significance of Communism in the 1930s is the proletarian emphasis that initiated the renaissance of people's culture. And it is Marxism, he believes, that leads to the restoration of the democratic tradition:

. . . Marxism is the heir to all the democratic traditions of mankind, and was intended to arm the people with modern weapons against the new and terrible weapons of modern finance capitalism.

If it was able to influence American writers so widely during the depression, this can only mean that Marxism was really able to help. . . . And the fact that there was present a living core of Marxist thought in America, ready to shape the thought of the intellectuals, is due to the presence of a mature and firm Communist movement . . . the legitimate child of American parents and grandparents such as Horace Greeley, Albert Brisbane, Eugene V. Debs, Bill Haywood, Jack London and Walt Whitman.[20]

For Gold the proletarian decade was not an accident; it was no artificially created culture. It emerged as a great movement "out of the heart of the American people." Marxism guided culture: "For democracy," he believed, "was dead in our literature in the Twenties. It was Marxism that revived it, and that saved the intellectuals by giving a democractic form and method to their inchoate protests." [21] In the first half of the decade, Gold argued, the Communists and left wing pioneers appeared to start the proletarian turn, and then the movement broadened into a national united front. The great cultural rebirth of the thirties, in his view, is grounded in the professional organizations that were unified around the progressive ideology and which produced the people's cultural movement. It was symbolized in literary terms by *The Grapes of Wrath* and *Native Son*. Its democratic soul was the Federal Arts Projects. [22]

V. J. Jerome's conclusion to *Intellectuals and the War* is equally ambiguous on the role of the Party in working with intellectuals. He reiterates the Browder position on freedom of artistic endeavor and notes Foster's analysis of the need to increase attention to the growing numbers of intellectuals in the Party. Jerome suggests that there is "still need for more systematic and concentrated effort in guiding the activities of professionals both inside the party and in their mass connections." And in the broadest terms he notes that Communism is a struggle against ugliness, an indictment of capitalism on aesthetic and economic grounds. He sees the socialist function in cultural terms as bringing art to the people in an intimate way. His final judgment, though, is far more rhetorical than analytical:

Challenging the bourgeois-fostered misconceptions of communism, the proletariat is creating great culture; it is by its historic nature a cultural class. As it advances in the struggle against capitalism and develops class consciousness, the proletariat brings forward intellectual forces from its own sons and daughters. . . .

. . . .

Against the sumptuous . . . universities there arise . . . workers' schools and study circles to arm the men of labor with the science of socialist transformation. Against the . . . press of the monopolies there is published, with the pennies of the dispossessed for its sole endowment, the humanly purposive, wholesome . . . workers' press. Against the statesmen, publicists and professional embellishers of the dying capitalist order arise propagandists of the people's advance and their emancipation; class-conscious scientists, educators, authors and artists—all the self-sacrificing and steadfast Communist intellectuals. [23]

At the same time, they wanted to defend the line for the people's democratic culture. Gold presented it in highly emotional terms, quoting Ma Joad's talk with son Tom at the end of *The Grapes of Wrath:* "We're the people." Jerome was more emphatic: "For every Hicks, or Bates, or

Sheean, there are hundreds of decent, modest intellectuals who stand guard at their posts despite reaction's offensive."[24]

What must be considered now is the specific development of the Party's work with intellectuals and culture in general and literature in particular. In the next several chapters we will consider the connection of intellectuals to the Party line, the proletarian phase (1930-35), and the aesthetics of the popular front. These chapters will provide the political context in which to understand the Party's approach to culture as it shifts away from the call to revolution in favor of anti-fascist politics.

CHAPTER 5

INTELLECTUALS
AND THE PARTY LINE

The CPUSA in the course of its five major conventions from 1930 to 1938 passed no resolution on the question of work with intellectuals, and the Central Committee issued no report directly on this matter. Only once, in 1938, after increasing numbers of professionals had been drawn to the Party, was there a brief analysis of such Party work. Throughout the decade there was no open discussion within the Party on this issue, yet there were more professionals than ever in the Party, and Communists were active in an increasing variety of cultural activities.

These activities included, in part, a daily cultural page in the *Daily Worker* published throughout most of the 1930s (and the creation of a magazine in the *Sunday Worker* devoted mainly to culture); a drive to build readership for political, cultural, and literary magazines of the left; book clubs, lecture tours, social groups, and art schools; and of course, the mass activities of the Writers' Congresses and the united front work on Spain and union building. The analysis below concentrates on the three Writers' Congresses to explain the Party position on intellectuals. These congresses offer the clearest expression of the contradiction between expanding Communist activity in culture and its limited political basis.

As we have seen, there is evidence to suggest that at the time of the First Writers' Congress there was a rather conscious attempt to bring cultural work into closer correspondence with the general political line of the Party—the Kharkov program. This first congress met before the shift to the united front when the line was still based on the call for a revolutionary way out of the crisis of the depression. The hope for the congress was to create a writers' organization tied to workers aesthetically through proletarian literature and politically through the LAW. The columns of the *Daily Worker* concerned with the congress constantly raised these two issues.

It is important to see that in addition to the well-documented anti-war and anti-fascism themes of the first congress, there was the plea for intellectuals to join more closely with workers; though no program was outlined, the LAW was certainly to be a beginning. The political problem of joining workers and intellectuals together in a common revolutionary program received considerable attention in the *DW*. The need for such unity was a common assumption, but there were doubts, too. Party spokesmen such as Mike Gold, Joseph North, and Alexander Trachtenberg were all somewhat cautious about the Party's ability to win over and keep the intellectuals. The intellectuals were viewed as disillusioned and disaffected, and as a group very susceptible to the appeal of fascism.[1] The proletarian flavor of the congress was, in part, an effort to push intellectuals into an alliance with workers. The *DW* editorial on the congress noted: "The writers at the Congress are not only united by their common opposition to fascist reaction and imperialist war, they are also united by their growing creative need to fuse their literary labor with the struggles and aspirations of the working class."[2]

However, the promulgation of the united front program in August 1935 cut short the efforts to create an organization to carry out the decisions of the First Congress. The approach to cultural activities at the First Congress was then criticized as too sectarian, and work in cultural affairs during the united front period, as we shall see, was shifted primarily to the politics of anti-fascism and union organizing of professionals. This shift took two years, but it was clearly articulated in the documents of the Second Congress of American Writers. Browder's speech, as noted, was its keynote. But Edwin Seaver, the *Sunday Worker* editor/book reviewer/writer, reporting on the congress in the *DW*, wrote quite directly on the concept of people's front and culture and is worth quoting:

It was a People's Front Congress from beginning to end, a congress in which a man of almost non-political training, like Ernest Hemingway, could cooperate fully with an avowed Communist like Joseph Freeman. A Congress in which Socialists, Communists, Liberals—all men and women of good will—felt the necessity of making a common stand against the scourge of fascism, the black and brown death that threatens the very existence of democratic culture. . . .

The road ahead is clear for widespread organization for the whole field of American writing. The presence of Archibald MacLeish, Ernest Hemingway, Donald Ogden Stewart, and Walter Duranty on the same platform at Carnegie Hall is an indication of what lies ahead. . . for the National League of American Writers.[3]

Seaver suggested that the political unanimity at this congress resulted from the lessons of Spain and Ethiopia, which revealed the true nature of fascism. Under the united front the essential political demand placed on writers was to defend civilization against a vicious and destructive force. He reported that the leading Party of opposition to fascism was the CP, and apparently that was taken for granted by the participants: the political discussions about the relationship to the working class so prominent at the First Congress were absent here. As Seaver explains:

There is no intention, nor any desire, that all the various writers in the league should maintain unanimity with regard to aesthetic objectives. Let there be as many schools of writing as the writers wish, and the more the merrier. But on certain basic, all-essential political aims there is and must be unanimity. Boiled down, these aims are concerned entirely with the defense of culture and with the formation of a genuine People's Front among our writers to bolster that defense.[4]

Organizationally, the LAW was restructured to accelerate the unification of all cultural workers in their respective labor unions, guilds, or associations to keep in step with the whole "progressive" American labor movement. The league was now to be a national group, with autonomous regional units handling the local issues. The Second Congress marks the beginning of the concerted drive toward unionization of the professions. The building of the united front in cultural areas was rather slow in the two years between the Seventh Comintern Congress and the Second Writers' Congress, but the changes were discernible: the *New Masses* was changed to a mainly political weekly for middle class intellectuals concentrating on Spain and fascism (and rebuttals on the trials), only secondarily concerned with culture and aesthetics. The JRC were phased out, but the JRC magazines—e.g., *Anvil* and *Partisan Review*—became the center of the proletarian literary movement of the transition period.[5] The Far West writers' group was organized to begin work with screen writers.[6] The cultural page of the *DW* was expanded and regularized with its primary focus movie, theatre, and book reviews. And the work within the Federal Arts projects was initiated.

The success of the people's front for culture is no better revealed than at the conclusion of the Second Congress when the Hollywood humorist Donald O. Stewart was elected president of the league and Van Wyck Brooks, Malcolm Cowley, Meridel Le Sueur, Erskine Caldwell, Upton Sinclair, Langston Hughes, Ernest Hemingway, and Archibald MacLeish were elected vice presidents. The eclectic politics of the united front is reflected in the five works selected for awards as "the most socially significant of the year": John Dos Passos, *The Big Money;* Joseph Freeman,

An American Testament; Carl Sandburg, *The People, Yes;* John Howard Lawson, *Marching Song;* and Van Wyck Brooks, *The Flowering of New England.*[7]

The work begun in 1937 climaxed at the Third Writers' Congress held in New York during the first week of June 1939. The speeches, discussions, and resolutions of this Third Congress have an especially ironic sound, coming as they do just moments before the announcement of the pact. Yet the Third Congress is an excellent case history of the politics of the democratic front. The call to the congress and its program clearly shows the emphasis on protection of democratic culture through the unity of progressive, anti-fascist writers functioning in the traditional literary fields (fiction and theatre), in the new mass media, and in the New Deal arts projects. Cultural work under the banner of the democratic front means progressive writers offering socially conscious themes to mass audiences. The slant of the discussions was "the defense of a free world in which writers can function." The call to the congress listed other discussion topics:

The defense of democracy in the United States, cooperation of this country with other nations and peoples opposed to fascism—including the Soviet Union, which has been the most consistent defender of peace; cooperation with writers exiled from the fascist countries; support for the anti-fascist policies of the present administration; support for labor unions; cooperation among all democratic and progressive forces; opposition to race prejudice, to attacks on social legislation, and to efforts to cripple or abolish the federal arts projects. . . .[8]

The congress was structured to concentrate on craft and technical problems, with sessions on radio writing, screen writing, poetry, literary criticism, drama, and general business problems of writers. The Third Congress was a professional writers' congress in the strictest sense and was the least overtly political of the three. The expansion of professional opportunities and the need for union and contractual protection dominated the discussions. The congress demonstrated the Party's success in organizing progressive forces in the cultural field. But unfortunately it also revealed how diluted the Party political program had become: in democratic front terms, the cultural workers were now the indispensable allies of the broad masses of people in the struggle against reaction and for democratic rights.

Samuel Sillen, the *New Masses* cultural commentator, reporting on the Third Congress, noted that there was no longer a need to discuss the question of the connection between art and politics because the events of the recent past had shown writers that all social phenomena are distinctly political. He offered this criticism of the First Congress:

> But the 1935 congress had serious limitations which were inevitable at
> the time. It represented a small though militant minority of American
> writers. It had to consume much of its energies arguing the elementary but
> then narrowly accepted truth that there is an intimate connection between
> politics and art. The congress had only the beginnings of the new social
> movement to give substance to its discussions. . . . Its social program was
> limited by the partial development of the democratic movement in the
> country.[9]

According to Sillen, the First Congress failed to deal with the need
for an expanded audience and with the serious economic problems of
authors. But the Third Congress registered remarkable gains in six areas.
First, with the membership of the LAW at 750, the delegates to the Third
Congress represented a majority of "leading" American writers: "These
writers are united in their determination to defend our tradition of democratic culture. Their ultimate goals, as writers and as citizens, may differ,
but they are bound together by a common loyalty to the democratic
idea." [10] Second, there was no need to discuss politics. Sillen quoted
Vincent Sheean's speech in which Sheean suggested that writers now
understood that all phenomena during periods of great social change are
political to some degree. Sillen suggested that because the congress was
united so strongly on the platform of anti-fascism there was no need to
expend energy arguing the issue of politics and literature. The congress
"could therefore concentrate on the practical literary implications of this
connection." Third, the struggle throughout the decade for "social
literature" had been won. The best writing in America in 1939—such as
Steinbeck's *The Grapes of Wrath,* Wright's *Uncle Tom's Children,* the
screenplay *Juarez,* and Robert Sherwood's *Abe Lincoln in Illinois*—which
might have been labeled political or propagandistic in the early part of
the decade, was by then readily accepted as militant affirmations of
our democracy.

The need to expand the audience for progressive literature was reflected
in the sessions on radio and screen writing. These discussions on the mass
media represented the fourth achievement.

Fifth was the concern over the economic problems of writers. Resolutions were adopted to join in closer cooperation the LAW and the
Authors League and to maintain the Federal Writers' Project. It should
be noted that the Tenth Party Convention passed a resolution in support
of the Pepper-Coffee bill to establish a permanent Federal Arts Program.
The Party called for support of the bill because it would insure the continued development of the cultural movement as part of the democratic

front. The Party urged a campaign for its passage to tie the cultural movement to other aspects of the progressive people's front.[11]

And sixth, Sillen pointed to the social program in support of democracy which reflected "the maturity of the progressive movement as a whole."[12]

Of the six areas of advancement, none was more prized than the gains made in Hollywood in the movie industry. It provides a good example of the fusion of anti-fascist politics, economic organization, defense of democratic culture, and cultivation of a mass audience. The LAW's Hollywood chapter summarized this work at a two-and-one-half-hour major session of the Third Congress.[13] The report on cinema, "The Screen As a Democratic Force," noted that movies had developed into a major industry requiring massive amounts of capital to sustain the production of modern films and at the same time needing the skills of thousands of talented workers. This had provided the opportunity to organize workers in Hollywood on a progressive basis to achieve economic security from the monopoly banking interests in control of Hollywood and to work for the development of a social cinema. The report said that "through trade union activity and extensive political and progressive organization Hollywood has become a vital center of democratic action."[14]

Strong unions, the report concluded, were the primary battle in defense of a free cinema: "Mechanized entertainment (motion picture, radio, television) holds the possibilities of a vast popular culture. But the control of that culture is not vested in the will of the people. The forces working for reaction are well aware of this."[15] Furthermore, Hollywood was a focal point in the struggle of democracy against reaction; and fighting for wages, copyrights, and royalties had helped to establish a true social cinema.

The significance of the Party work in Hollywood is further revealed in a four-part series in the *New Masses* published during the summer of 1939. The articles, written by Joseph North and Ella Winter, discuss the political, economic, trade union, and cultural aspects of Hollywood. In the first article Joseph North analyzes the development of Hollywood both as a major industrial center dominated by Wall Street financiers and as a cultural center of social cinema. As North stated, the Wall Street man wants his profit and the Main Street man wants reality—symbolized for North by the movies *Juarez* and *Confessions of a Nazi Spy*.[16]

In his second article North explains the basis of social cinema as the progressive organization of creative cultural workers fighting fascism and building unions. Why he asks, was *Juarez* possible?

Add all these factors up: a middle-of-the-road President; his New Deal support; the existence of the CIO; an organized movie industry; the stimulus to organization with the existence of the Wagner Act and the NLRB; a world teetering about the abyss of world war; the growing organization of film audiences and the increasing articulateness of movie-goers, stir all these ingredients together—and add the significant fact that the boy-meets-girl movies haven't been paying so well lately. Add the fact too that anti-labor pictures have been magnificent flops; and you begin to get to the truth.[17]

North traces the development of the organizing of Hollywood through the Anti-Nazi League in 1935 to the Motion Picture Artists Committee to Help Loyalist Spain in 1936, to the organizing of screen writers, directors, and a variety of smaller craft unions in 1937. In 1938 the Motion Picture Democratic Committee formed to work against the incumbent Republican (reactionary) Governor Frank Merriam. And in 1938 an effort was started to organize audiences in a group called the Associated Film Audiences.[18]

In the context of the popular front Third Congress, cinema is the art form for harmonizing the discords of people through the unity of workers and audience. Support of social cinema reflects directly the Communist equation of defense of people's democratic culture as the progressive political force. The people's democratic front can battle, in North's terms, the moguls of Wall Street. Therefore, radicalism in the movies of the 1930s became simply "people's" cinema: *The Informer, Emile Zola, Mr. Deeds Goes to Town, Our Daily Bread*, and the New Deal documentaries of Pare Lorenz, *The River*, and *The Plow That Broke the Plains*. The high point of the decade was the cinematic adaptation of *The Grapes of Wrath*.[19]

The Third Congress also devoted considerable attention to economic issues of professional writers in all categories—literary, magazine, radio, and screen.[20] In a memo on the trade union question, John Howard Lawson made the connection between unionism and democratic culture:

> The social and cultural objectives of the League of American Writers can be greatly aided by the extension of economic organization. A strong trade union is the *best guarantee* that writers will have the security, the protection from pressure or discrimination, the freedom of expression, which are essential for the growth of a democratic culture.
>
> I believe that the League . . . should offer active aid to the Authors' League's program of organization.
>
> . . . .
>
> The day is approaching when "Authors' League Shop" will cover the whole writing profession. When that day comes, the cultural and social influence of American writers will be enormously strengthened.[21]

The congress's Saturday general session was devoted to the business problems of writers. Albert Maltz spoke on the necessity of forming a massive trade union for all writers under the auspices of the Authors Guild section of the Authors League. Similar arguments were made on behalf of screen and radio writers. The measure of success for such organizing was the Dramatists Guild, which had secured an industry-wide basic agreement on advance payments, percentages, control of material, regulation of motion picture sale, etc., as early as 1926.[22]

At the height of the popular front in 1937 there appeared to exist the real beginning of a progressive cultural academy, an idea that Henry Hart suggested after the reorganization of the LAW at the Second Congress. He wanted a mass cultural organization with ties to the masses and some real influence—i.e., a progressive replacement for the stodgy American Academy of Arts and Letters. Of course, the pact broke the popular front and the possibility of such an academy, though the screen and radio writers remained very strong and cohesive throughout much of the forties.

Donald O. Stewart at the conclusion to his book on the Third Congress, *Fighting Words,* demonstrates, as I see it, that beneath the unity of this democratic front was, from a Marxist perspective, a fuzzy and insubstantial politics:

My faith is in the sound judgment of the people, provided they are allowed to know the facts. My hope is in the integrity of the American writers, whose duty it is to see that the people know the facts. That is the aim of culture, and that is the importance of its defense. That is the responsibility of the writer, and the problem is not national. The American writer is not alone. Writers from many other lands are allied in the struggle; many came to the congress to offer their help. Thomas Mann of Germany, Eduard Benes of Czechoslovakia, Louis Aragon of France, Sylvia Townsend Warner of England. . . . All came to bear witness to the fact that the defense of American culture is synonymous with the defense of all culture, and that the enemy is not any nation but an evil spirit in that nation, which would drown out the voices of the many in the interest of the voices of the few. It is an International Army, and it marches forward to the struggle in the knowledge that the defense of culture is the defense of all Mankind.[23]

One final estimation of the Party and the popular front is offered in two separate essays early in 1941. On the occasion of the thirtieth anniversary of the *New Masses,* Samuel Sillen (now Hicks's replacement as chief literary critic) noted that hundreds of leading intellectuals had appeared in the *New Masses* during its three decades of publication, and each writer "contributed to the magazine at the period of his healthiest and most forthright work—at the period. . .when he most faithfully reflected the life and aspirations of the people."

Whoever seeks to understand the appearance of *The Grapes of Wrath* and *Native Son*, of *Waiting for Lefty* and *Black Pit*, of *The Cradle Will Rock* and *Ballad for Americans*, must trace their genesis through the pages of the magazine. . . . American writers found *New Masses* a natural rallying ground. There they found an audience not for escapism but for uncompromising realism; there they found a point of view which provided work for the present and hope for the future. . *New Masses* was the workshop of proletarian literature in the thirties. At the end of the decade it stood prepared to defend a realistic and democratic culture against spiritual warlords like MacLeish and Mumford.[24]

Earl Browder (just prior to his entering Atlanta prison for a passport violation) suggested that it was no longer necessary for people to be Communists to come to the Party: "All they have to be is honest and decent and they have no other place to go." He added that even though America was swamped in a "great wave" of reaction and even though the Party was leading a rather small group of fighters for democracy, there was still great hope. "We represent the American search for truth; we represent the American tradition of democracy, of government of, by and for the people. We represent honest thought and culture; we represent the search for beauty; we represent the creative power of the masses. And that is why the future belongs to us."[25]

In my view, Communists working in the area of culture learned to become excellent defenders of socially conscious culture—fiction, poetry, theatre, reportage, and cinema—and builders of professional trade unions. But it is clear that they were not, as I and others define it, revolutionary Marxists. In the next three chapters we will see how the confusion over politics helped to undermine the attempt to build a Marxist approach to literature and art. One should note, however, that the relationship of revolution to reform was complex and difficult and that the relationships between Marxist doctrine and mass work and Marxist proletarian internationalism and the national traditions of a given country, do not lend themselves to formulas. As I see it, the CPUSA erred by losing a class and revolutionary perspective.

CHAPTER 6

THE POLITICS
OF THE PARTY LINE
IN THE 1930s

In the previous two chapters the general contours of the Party's approach to intellectuals and culture have been discussed. However, an accurate interpretation of Party work in culture cannot be divorced from an analysis of its general political line as the Party shifted away from the call to proletarian revolution after August 1935. As I have suggested, the Party's effort in culture was weakened by the failure to maintain a specific, independent identity as revolutionary Communists, but this weakness was really part of the larger political dilemma of the 1930s.

During the 1933-35 period the world Communist movement was confronted with an unprecedented crisis. The revolutionary third period policies within the Comintern proved disastrous, leading to narrow sectarian parties unable to grow and to resist the rise of fascism. This weakness was revealed in the dramatic crushing of the German CP, the largest CP outside of the Soviet Union. The Seventh Congress of the Comintern met in July and August 1935 to confront the threat of fascism and the weakened position of the CPs around the world. The main report to the congress was delivered by Georgi Dimitrov, hero of the Reichstag fire conspiracy trial and then secretary general of the Comintern. The report called for a united front against fascism. This was a major shift in line because it demanded an alliance with all political parties (even including the previously despised Social Democrats), workers' organizations, and liberal progressive forces. The Comintern was to attach no other condition to unified action than that it be directed against fascism.[1]

Dimitrov's speech gave political primacy to the attack on fascism and to mass organizing based on support of liberal democracy, expansion of workers' reforms under democracy, and defense of the Soviet Union. The call to proletarian revolution became, after this shift in line, little more than rhetoric. Dimitrov recognized the need for independent work by the Communist Parties but argued that the immediate problem was to preserve popular liberties and democratic rights in opposition to advancing fascist movements supported by monopoly and finance capitalists. To combat the powerful threat of fascism, Dimitrov for the Comintern advocated "both short and long term agreements providing for *joint action with Social Democratic Parties, reformist trade unions and other organizations of the toilers* and against the class enemies of the proletariat."[2]

The Dimitrov speech provides the basic political analysis for the developments of the united front policy in America, though of course its practical implementation was organized within the CPUSA. The traditional Bolshevik demand for the dictatorship of the proletariat was redefined. In concluding his address, Dimitrov gave the following advice to parties in the West:

We want our Parties in the capitalist countries to come out and act as *real political parties of the working class,* to become in actual fact *a political factor* in the life of their countries, to pursue at all times *an active Bolshevik policy and not confine themselves to propaganda and criticism, and bare appeals to struggle for proletarian dictatorship.*[3]

The specific approach for the United States, developed by the Comintern and the American CP, was the attempt to form a workers' and farmers' party that would be truly anti-fascist without being anti-Communist, a "proletarian" party which would fight the banks (and all such enemies of the people), and which would demand progressive social legislation for workers and unemployed, land for black and white sharecroppers, cancelation of farmers' debts, equality for Negroes, rights for war veterans, and support for the interests of the liberal professions, small businessmen, and artisans.[4]

The CPUSA under the leadership of Earl Browder turned its efforts to creating a mass political movement under the slogan "Americanize the Party." The effort to organize a labor party failed, with Communists instead rallying behind the C.I.O. leadership and ultimately the New Deal. The political theme of the post-1935 period became the demand to defend the rights of the people. The masthead of the *DW* changed in September 1936 from "Central Organ of the CPUSA (Section of the Communist International)" to "People's Champion of Liberty, Progress, Peace and Prosperity." This new direction for the Party was also reflected in Browder's slogan "Communism Is Twentieth Century Americanism," a term coined shortly before the Seventh Congress.

In December 1938, at the height of the popular front, Earl Browder wrote a brief retrospective essay for *The Communist* discussing American revolutionary traditions, using, as its central theme, "Communism is Twentieth Century Americanism." [5] Though he was mainly concerned with showing how the slogan had been abused and applied too uncritically, there is a very succinct restatement of the original united front policy. In the essay Browder argues that the Party is the central bulwark in defense of democracy against the encroachments of fascist forces of reaction.

The concept of "Good Americans," in the sense of the national democratic and revolutionary traditions, embraces the whole progressive majority of the people, and, further, extends to a degree among the conservative masses insofar as they show capacities of resistance to the modern forces of reaction. We Communists, taking our place as an integral sector of the progressive and democratic camp, claim the common title of "Good Americans," and further add to it a claim that our particular principles and program embody the *future* developments of our country.[6]

Browder reemphasizes the need to make alliances with all progressive forces (trade unions, government, and even progressive non-monopoly capitalists). In this view, class struggle has been redefined in the U.S. into a battle between monopoly reaction and farm-labor democracy.[7] To build the united front, the Party worked to take the lead in all short-term reform struggles. The goal after 1935 was to make the Party a mass organization—i.e., the vanguard party of the masses of the American people. In this view, the people's front provided the precondition for socialism, by defeating fascism and building the mass militant organizations which would change the people's consciousness. The united front strategy is a sharp departure and needs to be contrasted with the Party program in force up through August of 1935.

The most rhetorically stirring and visionary statement of the Party program for the pre-1935 period was William Z. Foster's *Toward Soviet America*. Outlining the process for applying the Soviet model to America, he attacked the Socialist party, the A.F.L., and the New Deal as agents of the bourgeoisie, labeling the leaders Norman Thomas, Mathew Woll, William Green, John L. Lewis, and Franklin Roosevelt "social fascists." He argued that the only way out of the crisis of the depression was the revolutionary road under the banner and leadership of the Communist Party: "The Communist Party bases its activity upon the principles of the class struggle, both with regard to its everyday struggles and its ultimate revolutionary goal."[8]

Foster's book is important for the clarity with which the call to revolution is made, but on the level of practice it is not particularly revealing or self-critical. A much more accurate depiction of the Party program in the pre-1935 period is found in a statement issued by the Central Committee after a special conference called to discuss why the Party in the middle of the worst depression in American history (with so much spontaneous unrest) had not become a mass revolutionary Party. The document, "An Open Letter to All Members of the Communist Party," summarizes the Party program for the early 1930s and shows the failures, pointing to the necessary changes needed to create a mass revolutionary Party.[9] The Open Letter clearly represents the militant, mass action, non-opportunist line of the revolutionary pre-1935 period. It reflects the Bolshevik ideas of a proletarian party tied directly to workers through factory units and Communist fractions in the trade unions; this was the tactic of "united front from below" to win workers to the Party while attacking the socialist and reformist trade union "misleaders." It was an unsuccessful approach.

The Extraordinary Party Conference was called in July 1933 because the program for connecting the Party to the working class in major industries (steel, auto, textile, etc.) through the forming of factory units (or nuclei as they were then called) had not developed. The Party was growing, but its membership was top-heavy with unemployed workers—a problem not limited to the U.S.[10] The Open Letter was issued in response to a real and recognized dilemma. That the crisis of the depression intensified the class struggle was demonstrated by increasing worker militancy (strikes and marches), and the Party was desperately trying to respond by organizing both the employed and unemployed. But the primary success was with the unemployed workers, leaving the Party poorly prepared in the factories.[11]

The Extraordinary Conference was designed to create a program to soften the contradiction between the enormous potential for growth and the meager results. Party growth was substantial: 9,219 in 1931, 14,474 in 1932, 19,165 in 1933 and 31,500 in 1936.[12] But there remained the persistent problems of high numbers of unemployed workers, of too few factory units, and of a turnover of more than 75 percent (the Party term was fluctuation).[13] In the Open Letter the self-criticism of the Party's weaknesses was sharp and on target:

The rise of the strike movement, the mass action of the unemployed, the increasing opposition within the A.F. of L. against the bureaucracy, the various movements which are growing at a tempestuous pace among the poor farmers and ruined middle farmers, the movements among the masses of petty bourgeoisie in the cities and the toiling intelligentsia . . . all these factors indicate that the revolutionary upsurge is gaining momentum. But in spite of the radicalization of the masses of workers, the Party has not developed into a revolutionary *mass Party* of the Proletariat, even though it can point to a number of achievements in its work, such as the

Detroit strike, in the Hunger Marches, in the veterans' movement and in the Farmers' Conference.[14]

The central decision at the Conference was to move ahead with organizing a mass trade union movement built on small factory nuclei in the large mass production industries. It was a decision which reflected the Bolshevik idea of a Party with a firm, large, and flexible proletarian base unified by the principle of democratic centralism and ready to lead strikes and protests:

. . . The center of gravity of Party work must be shifted to the development of the *lower organizations,* the factory nuclei, local organizations and street nuclei. It goes without saying that it is our task to place ourselves at the head of every movement which breaks out spontaneously in the country, and to lead such movements, or where reformist leaders stand at the head of a movement, to work for the building of fighting organs of the masses, independent of bureaucrats, in order to aid the masses in the exposure and replacement of the reformist leaders. But unless we tenaciously concentrate our work on the most important industrial centers, we cannot build up a stable Party and revolutionary trade union movement, capable of resisting all blows and persecutions by the bourgeoisie.[15]

The primary allies in this struggle are the poor and small farmers and the masses of Negroes. As for the middle class white collar workers and intellectuals, they too might be won over or at least neutralized in the struggle between workers and capitalists.[16]

The Party program was reformulated at the conference on eight basic principles: (1) to fight against wage cuts and reductions in real wages; (2) to connect the wage fight with the efforts to secure unemployment insurance and to fight against exploitation of the unemployed in New Deal work projects; (3) to demand cancelation of farmers' debts and end exploitation of sharecroppers; (4) to protect veterans' disability payments; (5) to struggle for equal rights for Negroes and for black belt self-determination; (6) to end political suppression; (7) to fight German fascism; and (8) to protect the Soviet Union against a new imperialist war.[17]

As demonstrated by Party statistics, the Open Letter program to organize shop nuclei in the major industries and to cultivate proletarian leadership at the lower levels of the Party was never fulfilled. Much of the problem was external. Organizing mass production industries in the early 1930s was dangerous business and was often carried out secretly in tiny groups of two or three workers. This significantly increased the hardships of issuing shop newspapers and leaflets and of distributing the *DW*—also part of this campaign.

But the most intriguing aspect of the 1933-34 period was violent workers' struggles and growing strike waves. While Communist cadres concentrated their efforts on these events, they did not use the opportunity to organize nuclei on the basis of the Party's program. While Communists became more active in actual strikes and militant battles, they did not build the workers' units in the factories at the same time. Though the later trade union work of the Party became widespread and influential, with Communist cadres in large measure responsible for the successful C.I.O. drive in the latter half of the decade, that organizing effort was never developed on the basis of a revolutionary political program.[18]

Recruiting drives were expanded, and to accommodate the expected sharp increase in Party members the bureaucratic structure was tightened and reorganized. Party-wide discussions on methods to reduce fluctuation and to maintain interest of new members dominated this period. It is easy to criticize the Party for its overemphasis on organizational questions— especially if the intent is to show a monolithic and regimented Party. But the concern with structure cannot be isolated from the program. The tightening process in the bureaucracy is a direct response to the Open Letter. Many of the weaknesses of the Party are traceable to this restructuring. The Party became, as I see it, overly concerned with numbers and not the quality (in a political sense) of members. It became infatuated with a smooth-running bureaucracy with prompt dues collection and dissemination of orders and programs. While the desire to build a Party from the bottom was certainly present, the result was the reverse. The program for organization and structure was published in 1935 as an extension of the Open Letter. It was J. Peter's *The Communist Party: A Manual on Organization.*

To join the Party one had to be eighteen years of age and accept the program and statutes of the Communist International and the CPUSA. Officially one also had to be active in a Party unit, pay dues regularly, and abide by Party discipline. In practice, however, dues payment became the central qualification. And recruiting was not undertaken seriously or consistently, occurring too often at mass rallies and demonstrations where applications were circulated. While the organizing of shop nuclei languished, the circulation of the *DW* was pushed to 70,000 by 1935, the Young Communist League was developed, and alliances to fight fascism were built, especially among the middle class professionals.

Browder discussed this program at the Thirteenth Plenum of the ECCI where he described the plan for fulfilling the Open Letter. According to Browder's report, the Party planned an eight-part campaign: (1) to recruit the more immediate Party supporters; (2) to build the *DW* into a mass circulation daily; (3) to step up work in building revolutionary trade unions and opposition in the reformist unions; (4) to increase the YCL activities and recruitment; (5) to organize the unemployed; (6) to advance the work in agriculture; (7) to be more active in organizing women; and (8) to build the fight against war and fascism.[19]

But by the time of the Eighth Party Convention in April 1934 the membership problems remained. The Party had grown in terms of absolute numbers, but the shop units in basic industry were meager: 154 units with 1,323 members up from 68 shop units with 459 at the time of the July 1933 Extraordinary Conference. The majority of shop units were in light industries and small shops, with 80 percent of the Party in neighborhood street units. As the united front period arrived, the CPUSA was composed mainly of unemployed, non-union workers oriented to light industry. Its base in the heavy industries was terribly small.[20]

"We are still a ridiculously small Party," Earl Browder said in his first major public address after the Seventh Comintern Congress. "There are 50,000 workers immediately surrounding our Party, ready and fit to become Party members. We keep them out by our sectarian inner-Party life. . . ."[21] Here was the keynote for the shift to the united front for the CPUSA. The work to increase membership, to build *DW* circulation, and to gain trade union influence continued, but the political basis for this activity changed. The call for anti-fascist unity, trade union democracy, and immediate social reforms made recruiting easier and far more successful, though the nagging problems of very high fluctuation and rigid bureaucracy remained. Communists, as the Party's periphery expanded greatly, became even more self-conscious of the fact that actual membership lagged far behind its potential. Membership requirements were eased and new recruits were brought in on the politics of the popular front, not on the explicit call for revolution and dictatorship of the proletariat. While the early discussions and pronouncements about the united front contained many references to the need for the Party to maintain an independent presence, it did not.[22]

At the Tenth Party Convention in May 1938, the leadership boasted 75,000 registered members and 20,000 in the YCL—a 100 percent gain since 1936. Though this increase is substantial, it obscures the central dilemma of the popular front period. A program was never advanced to build the Party while working, at the same time, in the mass movements of the latter half of the decade—especially in the C.I.O. *The Party Organizer,* in the period from 1936 to its last issue in August 1938, was devoted almost entirely to questions of recruiting. Yet the articles devoted to analysis consistently reflect the fact that Party workers were forced to devote most of their energy to the mass organizations, which left little time for Party building.

Recent research on the question of Communists in the trade union movement in the 1930s substantiates this weakness. For example, James R. Prickett challenges and refutes (with evidence) the major cold war anti-Communist myths of trade union subversion.[23]

According to Prickett, the C.I.O. succeeded because Communists acted as militant trade unionists dedicating themselves to unionization of the basic industries.[24] He believes that about 20 percent of the Party's members worked in basic industry. He estimates that while the Party was active in its union work in the late 1930s and early 1940s about 100,000 workers in basic industry joined. Though he admits that many dropped out, his evidence suggests that these workers continued to be friendly and to support the Party's work.[25] The basic reason for the high dropout rate was ". . .the party's failure to make the necessity of a Communist Party clear." [26] Furthermore, he argues that the failure to recruit even more workers cannot be laid to workers' conservatism or anti-Communism but directly to the Party's strategy and politics: ". . . party activists frequently neglected to combine recruiting with other activities such as union building, organizing community groups and leading strikes." [27] But this must be understood in terms of a rather weird political contradiction. Participation in the mass organizations was far more exciting and less dangerous than work as a CP member. Party work tended to be dull but, given the persistent oppression, always more dangerous. In actuality, there was less risk in being part of the more active mass movement.

Prickett's research shows that the decision to build the C.I.O. as the leading progressive and working class organization without an independent and clear Communist voice led inevitably to the destruction of the Party. Prickett is concerned with explaining the Party's defeat in the post-World War 2 period and believes that the gradual accommodation with the C.I.O. leadership under the popular front was in the long run the root cause. His conclusions are worth quoting at length:

. . . Communists were defeated in the postwar period because their position in the labor movement rested on such a weak foundation. That weak foundation was not the result of working class conservatism, but rather of the party's failure to put itself forward aggressively at a time when its prestige was high. . . .the failure to maintain party fractions inside the unions, the abandonment of shop papers published by Communist workers, the failure to maintain a Communist position independent of the position of the union leadership or the caucus in which the Communists were included. . . . [28]

The Party was open to attack, according to Prickett, because the abandonment of the call for socialism led, unfortunately, to a reluctance to build the Party during the popular front:

. . .the Communist Party lost those attributes which should distinguish a Communist Party from other political formations. Communists abandoned the struggle for socialism, gave their support to the New Deal, and made no serious or consistent attempt to challenge liberal ideology. They abolished the institution which enabled them to play a coordinated role within the labor movement—the party fraction—and stopped publishing shop papers. . . . As unionists, they were far superior to their anti-Communist counterparts but they were poor Communists.[29]

The Party's own analysis of registration and recruiting for 1938, prepared for the Tenth Convention, reaches similar conclusions. The number of shop units did not increase from 1936 to 1938. Instead, the emphasis was switched to larger industrial units; some 582 units were built and 12,000 workers were recruited. The street or neighborhood units had 14,000 more members than in 1936, but the number of units had not appreciably increased. There were a mere 5,000 Negro Party members by the Tenth Convention. The most significant advance was made in the recruiting of working women into the Party: about 25 percent of the members were women, representing a doubling from 10,000 to 20,000 in the two-year period.

The report noted a significant advance in the number of members active in trade unions. By January 1938 27,000 Communists were in trade unions, and if the number active in the Workers Alliance were added, then 50 percent of the Party membership was in the trade union movement. Fluctuation in the two-year period was still high, however, about 46 percent.

In commenting on the social composition of the membership, the analysis points to increasing numbers of professional and white collar members. The concern was to avoid a Party top-heavy with people not in basic industry—mainly a problem for the New York City units.[30]

It is clear that the Party failed to build a program on the Open Letter, and this failure was disastrous in the long run. The Party did not make a strong effort to maintain a separate identity, but rather submerged its program in the popular front. The work inside the unions (steel, auto, longshoremen, maritime, transportation, electrical, etc.) was primarily devoted to militant unionism. The decade-long efforts to issue shop papers and to work through Communist fractions were abandoned in 1939 as a gesture of cooperation and a tactic to "disarm" the anti-Communists. There was no concerted attempt to elect Communists to leadership positions through a rank-and-file campaign for workers' support. A similar strategy was established for the work of the Party in its other mass activities (Spain, the National Negro Congress, and the Workers Alliance) and also carried over into the cultural campaign.[31]

The popular front strategy was expanded at the Tenth Party Convention, on the assumption that the Party had become an active force in mass labor and progressive organizations. The CC proposed the creation of a "broad democratic front of all labor and progressive forces." This intermediary step of achieving a democratic front was suggested because a farm-labor party had not been formed.[32] This was, in essence, an alliance with progressive or left elements within the New Deal: "The democratic front is a democratic bloc of common action of all labor, progressive and democratic forces to fight against reaction and fascism, to maintain and extend democracy. . . . The democratic front under present conditions is the path to the establishment of the anti-fascist People's Front, is the policy to ensure the victory of democracy over fascism."[33]

The fight against fascism had assumed a broader political basis. It now included Roosevelt and other "progressive" democrats. And the issues held in common were peace, trade union rights, civil liberties, the fight for more jobs, and relief.

On the occasion of the twentieth anniversary of the CPUSA, Earl Browder sketched the history and development of the Party, arguing for the validity of the united front program. He saw the Tenth Convention as clearly fixing the CP as "the democratic party of the working class continuing the best American traditions while preparing for the socialist future." "We set ourselves the task to win the respect and allegiance of the majority of the American people, as the precondition for socialism in our country."[34] Browder asserts in this message that the history of the Party throughout the depression decade was a concerted effort to involve itself in the mass struggles of the "people." He points to the 1930-33 struggles in the unemployed movement, the strikes of the independent unions, and the veterans' bonus march, the sharp changes within the trade union movement in the 1933-36 period which had pushed the Party back inside of the A.F.L. and had helped to establish the C.I.O., and the Eighth Party convention, which initiated a campaign to revive American revolutionary traditions as part of an overall reinterpretation of American history. Browder also claims success in defeating the reactionary forces in the 1936 presidential election and the beginning of tentative alliances with progressive forces inside of the New Deal and the Democratic Party.

The title of Carl Sandburg's famous poem *The People, Yes* (1936), was symbolic of what had become the catchall phrase of the late 1930s. During the popular front the CPUSA became the self-proclaimed people's party. As William Z. Foster noted, "The more we dramatize—correctly, of course—the hardships and poverty of the people, the more we create a favorable public opinion for the people's democratic demands and the more difficult we make it for reaction. . . ."[35]

However, in my view, the politics of the united front was based on the false premise that anti-fascism could serve as a substitute for revolutionary Communism, and the rather extraordinary successes in building the progressive struggles in the latter half of the decade were misperceived as helping to build a revolutionary Communist Party. Though it grew to be an ubiquitous organization of 100,000 (including YCL) by the decade's end (from a fractured Party of 7,000 in 1930), it approached World War 2 with its Bolshevism thinned beyond recognition.

In the next two chapters the Party approaches to intellectuals and culture will be considered in the context of the general shift in Party politics from the call to proletarian revolution to the united front. However, before leaving the discussion of the general political line some comment must be made on the relationship of the CPUSA to the Comintern.

Too often the histories of the Party in America point to the shift of line in 1935 as evidence of dictatorship by Moscow, trying in some measure to prove that the CPUSA was in service to a foreign power. But this effort to show control does not help to uncover what the American Communists did and how successful they were in practice. It is true that American Communists never questioned the notion that the Comintern was the "general staff" of the world revolution. Throughout the decade the Americans never considered the Comintern a collective of equal parties.

Soviet leadership was accepted on the basis of its successful revolution, and the Leninist Bolshevik model was never criticized; in essence, it became the example for all revolutionary Communist Parties. The Soviets, as leaders of the world Communist movement, never allowed the International to become a partnership of equals in which differences and needs of various sections were considered, but neither were the Soviets narrowly dictatorial. The Comintern did articulate the new policy in 1935; however, it also offered very accurate and penetrating criticisms of organizational and political problems in the work of the CPUSA—a supportive function too often ignored in traditional histories. Ultimately, it is pointless to argue over the source of political ideas and strategy under which the Party operated in America. But it must be noted that the CPUSA's relationship with the Comintern in the 1930s is not best characterized as master/slave. Discussions, consultations, and disagreements were far more open and robust than generally acknowledged.

CHAPTER 7

THE PROLETARIAN PHASE
IN AMERICA

In the context of the Kharkov program, the First Writers' Congress, and the Open Letter, what was the political and organizational basis which the Party formulated to advance proletarian literature in the 1930-35 period? As we have seen, the evidence shows that the proletarian phase developed gradually from the Kharkov Conference. It required almost five years to fulfill the basic goal, which was to build a mass circulation cultural magazine while at the same time cultivating the proletarian JRC (and its literary magazines). The variety of tactics and ventures were responses to the American scene—not modeled on the Soviet Union. However, the overriding characteristic of this period was the distance that existed between Party politics in general and Party activity in culture and literature. This distance existed even though there was a rather clear program under the Kharkov principles and a high interest in proletarian writing.

The primary evidence of this separation is reflected in the fact that literary issues were not included in the central political documents of the period (i.e., National Convention resolutions or Central Committee reports). More significantly, cultural matters were not included as part of the 1933 Open Letter or discussed at the Extraordinary Conference. What should be acknowledged was the fact that there was a general correspondence between the revolutionary line of the Open Letter and the concept of proletarian literature as advocated in the *New Masses* and by Communist literary critics. The Open Letter line of building a mass party rooted in the working class and in the basic industries was reflected in literary activities in two *indirect* ways: first, building a mass audience, and second, raising class consciousness in that audience through revolutionary literature.

However, it must be clearly understood that this correspondence is derived inductively from a perusal of the political documents and the literary practice. *It is not derived from any published material produced by either Party leaders or literary critics.* There are no documents extant joining the issues of Open Letter politics and literary activity.

The closest connection between a national Party meeting and a meeting of a literary group occurred in June 1932 when the national nominating convention met in Chicago to select Foster and Ford and at the same time the JRC held its national meeting. One decision made at the JRC meeting was to involve writers in the election campaign through the creation of the Professional Groups for Foster/Ford (see chapter 3, above). However, this decision to involve writers and intellectuals in the election campaign had its roots in the Kharkov resolutions and not in the specific political considerations of the nominating convention.

A review of the documents of another important political event, the Eighth National Convention held in April 1934—the first since the Open Letter—also shows no discussion of the cultural program or its tie to the events of the previous year. And Browder's report to the convention on behalf of the CC is also empty. Further evidence of the distance between Party politics and cultural life emerges from the debates and controversies over the development of proletarian literature. Walter Rideout's rather complete study of statements made by the major Marxist and Party literary critics—Freeman, Gold, Kunitz, Seaver, and Rahv—indicates that the discussions were consistently literary and scholastic and rarely political or organizational.

Rideout reaches this conclusion after scrutinizing all aspects of the discussion over proletarian literature which began with Mike Gold's attack on Thornton Wilder in the fall of 1930 in the *New Republic* and stretched to the *Partisan Review* split with the Party in 1937. (Of course, after the shift to the united front and the revelations of the purge trials these disagreements turned hotly political.)[1]

For Rideout these literary debates were ultimately inconsequential, because when the line shifted in 1935 proletarian literature became the casualty of political expediency. Rideout believes that the Party killed proletarian literature:

Wherever one turns, then, for an explanation of the decline in the proletarian novel, one is ultimately brought back face to face with the political reversal contained in the People's Front. The maneuver . . . was an astute one from the standpoint of the Party. It brought Communism, if not Marxism, as closely into the mainstream of American development as Socialism had been brought in the years just before World War I; and liberals must acknowledge that the new Party line gave impetus to the movement for many much-needed reforms, even if at the same time the cooperation of the Left made the general movement more vulnerable to attack from the Right. In the course of that maneuver, however, *the proletarian novel was dumped without ceremony* : . . and with it went very probably the last opportunity for a radical fiction of any size in the United States out of Marxist doctrine.[2]

Rideout is correct, I think, in suggesting that the Party was highly influential in literary matters by 1935, but, as the discussion in the previous chapters demonstrated, there is little evidence to suggest that it had such a firm idea about the direct relationship between politics and literature. The Party leadership suggested a vague correspondence between support for the proletariat and closer bonds with the Party. In these discussions, by Marxist and Party literary critics as they worked out a definition of proletarian literature and culture, this distance is clearly revealed. Conspicuously absent from these debates is a discussion of the role of the Party as the political leader of cultural affairs.

For example, the most complete statement on the definition, development, and direction of proletarian literature in the U.S. by a Party spokesman is Joseph Freeman's introduction to the well-known literary collection *Proletarian Literature in the United States: An Anthology* (1935). For Freeman art has a very special function in the class struggle: in our contemporary life, he argues, the key social issues of the day are unemployment, strikes, the fight against war and fascism, and the struggle for revolution; these social experiences should become the primary influence on artistic creativity. When an artist understands the relationship between these social struggles and the strategic role of the proletariat, he will begin to produce revolutionary proletarian art.

Essentially, Freeman argues that the Party provides revolutionary leadership and gives the writer a higher political consciousness. Proletarian literature, in these terms, becomes the logical development of American literary realism, giving voice to previously ignored people and recording their lives in the style of realism—the observable fact. However, Freeman does not discuss the function of the Communist Party as the political leader of the proletarian literary movement, though he hints at its vanguard role:

Every writer creates not only out of his feelings, but out of his knowledge and his concepts and his will. However crude or unformulated or prejudiced his philosophy may be . . . it colors his works. The revolutionary movement in America—as in other countries—is developing a generation which sees the world through the illuminating concepts of revolutionary science. The feelings of the proletarian writer are molded by his experience, just as the bourgeois writer's feelings are molded by his experiences and the class theories which rationalize them.[3]

In what is considered to be the authoritative statement on proletarian literature, there is no discussion of the connection between the Party and literature. This is also reflected in all of the discussions over proletarian literature by critics, writers, and Party leaders. There is an identifiable pattern to these discussions: they are personal viewpoints, and explore the proletarian issue mainly on the literary level; they rarely analyze the role of the Party (in a Leninist sense) in literary matters or the general political line of the Party; and they reflect a panorama of viewpoints.[4]

What emerged, as Rideout accurately states, were two central tendencies: one, represented primarily in the *New Masses* under the leadership of Gold and Hicks, argued for a literature describing class struggle and supporting the proletariat. The second, representing the position of Philip Rahv, William Phillips, and Joshua Kunitz, wanted a literature of high artistic quality which would advance proletarian culture and not simply depict the class struggle.[5] What is seen in these discussions are the intellectual efforts of individual critics who debated the issues extensively and with remarkable toleration and openness for opposing ideas.

These discussions must also be understood in the context of significant growth in the acceptance of proletarian culture. And of course Party influence in cultural life also advanced. First, the *New Masses* was reorganized as a weekly addressed mainly to the middle class. Its circulation jumped from a meager 6,000 in 1933 to a respectable 25,000 in January 1935. The proletarian magazines published under the auspices of the JRC were finding new audiences.[6] Revolutionary writing was published not just in the left-oriented press but through bourgeois houses too. Left wing plays were finding producers and audiences as well. As Joseph Freeman noted in 1934, there was the beginning of a "vital revolutionary art." "Revolutionary literature and criticism," he announced happily, "are now out in the open. . . ."[7] The *DW* maintained a daily cultural page throughout this period, and with the advent of the *Sunday Worker* in 1936, edited by Joseph North, Al Richmond, Edwin Seaver, and James Allen, this interest in cultural activities was augmented by a Sunday magazine. Finally, there was the organizing of the First American Writers' Congress, which was suggested by Alexander Trachtenberg at the September 1934 JRC convention (see chapter 3, above).

It is often suggested that the politics of the proletarian phase was grounded in a harsh and dogmatic rhetoric. In culture the evidence shows a rather moderate and open style designed to encourage writers and artists to move left. For example, an important part of the struggle to convert the *New Masses* into a major cultural journal was the push to bring sympathetic fellow travelers closer to the magazine. As early as November

1932 Joseph Freeman in his report to the JRC was calling for a reorganization of the *New Masses* to reflect the advances of Communism, to be open to intellectuals as they move left, and of course, to encourage that movement.[8]

A similar note of moderation toward liberal sympathizers was sounded by A. B. Magil in late 1932. Magil wrote in the *New Masses* that it is wrong and snobbish to be pessimistic about the liberal writers, and that Communists should be particularly sensitive to the needs of this group. He warns comrades about being overly demanding.[9]

Writing two years later, in September 1934, Freeman notes a new openness in an essay that reviews the 1932-34 period: "Anyone has only to declare himself a 'fence-sitter' and he is embraced with open arms; our press is his and he can say anything he likes, however remote it may be from revolutionary thought. The abandonment of sectarianism has had a healthy effect; our literary movement has made great progress as a result of it. . . ."[10]

That same mood of moderation emerges in Joseph North's nostalgic retrospective on the *New Masses:* "We had purpose. We portrayed reality and we pursued a goal—the Marxist, socialist objective. We did so in prose, poetry, criticism, art, and that did *not* violate the judgment, the perception, the aesthetic, of the existent generation." [11] North characterized the orientation of the magazine as moderate. He likened it to a *New Republic* or *Nation* for the left, a complete political and cultural journal.[12]

Thus, the literary side of the discussions over proletarian culture shows a rather open and liberal attitude by the Communists toward dissenting opinions—except, of course, toward those in active conflict with the Party such as Eastman, Calverton, and Hook. There was little dictatorship by the primary literary spokesmen for the Party, and except for Browder's speech at the First Writers' Congress, virtual silence from the Party leadership. This disinterest was a function of their belief that intellectuals and writers were of small import in creating a mass revolutionary Communist Party, that they were politically fickle and unstable, and that their small numbers did not warrant heavy involvement. If one recalls that the First Congress included only 216 participants and the LAW reported only 125 members in November 1935, this attitude becomes somewhat more understandable. Interestingly, the Party documents for this period reveal no heavy campaign directed at drawing writers and intellectuals into the Party, and this is understandable in light of the Open Letter.

The program and plans for the *New Masses* and JRC based on the Kharkov resolutions, along with the call for proletarian revolutionary writing, helped to keep the literary movement in general alignment with the political line of the Party. And one may argue that the organizing of the First Writers' Congress was really an overt attempt to integrate literary work with the general political line.

Considering both the literary and political evidence of the proletarian phase, it seems clear that the Party did not fully exploit its prestige as revolutionary Communists in literary matters as its influence grew. It never offered a comprehensive program based on a clear political objective. The real advances made during this period of a relatively strong revolutionary line were obvious. But equally obvious is the fact that merely to have a group of serious Marxist literary critics who were Party members when the line was strong and sharp was not enough to generate an aesthetic. The necessary thoroughgoing discussion within the Party to weld literature to the general politics did not occur. Furthermore, the tentative political connections of the First Congress evaporated under the pressure of the popular front. As a matter of fact, it seems that what I see as the shrouding of the revolutionary Communist line was more easily accomplished during the popular front precisely because this connection had not been integrated earlier and the Marxist position on literary matters was left to individuals.

Ultimately, it is this separation which explains the problems and difficulties during the popular front and which provides the key to understanding the general attitude toward intellectuals (discussed in chapters 4 and 5, above). In the realm of culture, it is safe to state that the Party's ideology during the proletarian phase may have been militant and left but its practice was moderate.

In the next chapter I will analyze the aesthetics of the popular front. In the years after the shift to the united front, anti-fascist politics and people's culture without any independent Communist voice failed to integrate and unify literature with revolutionary politics.

CHAPTER 8

THE AESTHETICS
OF THE POPULAR FRONT

> they have clubbed us off the streets they are
> stronger they are rich they hire and fire poli-
> ticians the newspapereditors the old judges the
> small men with reputations the college presidents . . .
> they have built the electricchair and hired the
> executioner to throw the switch
> all right we are two nations
> America our nation has been beaten by strangers . . .
> but do they know that the old words of the immi-
> grants are being renewed in blood and agony tonight.
> . . . .
>
> the men in the deathhouse made the old words new
> before they died. . . .
> we stand defeated America.[1]

These famous bitter words about the executions of Sacco and Vanzetti, memorializing one of the great catalytic political tragedies of the 1920s, were in large part responsible for awarding Dos Passos's *The Big Money* the label of best novel of the year at the Second Writers' Congress.[2] This award offers one small but enlightening guidepost to the aesthetics of the popular front. Because at the end of the novel when the reader is anguishing over the murder of Sacco and Vanzetti, Dos Passos begins what eventually became a lifelong career of attacking the Communist Party.

One cannot read through the more than 1,300 pages of the *U.S.A.* trilogy without being drawn up short by the repudiation of the Party. The final sections of the novel find Ben Compton cast out as a renegade, Don Stevens turned into a Stalinist automaton, and the déclassé fellow traveler Mary French frantically running to yet another meeting in support of the striking workers. Yet the reviews on the left were essentially positive, and the award at the Second Congress was given in recognition of its artistic excellence. Of course, Dos Passos had always been cultivated by the Communists, who ranked him near the top of the proletarian and socially conscious artists in America. This was done even though Dos Passos's disaffection from Communism began sharply in February 1934 when he protested the Party's action at a large meeting in Madison Square Garden.[3]

But the real break with the CP came, however, not over literature but over politics. Dos Passos's support of the Dewey investigations into the Moscow trials brought a sharp attack by Mike Gold in his *DW* column of February 17, 1937, a criticism that culminated in mid-summer when Gold devoted a column to Dos Passos's ever-changing politics. Concentrating on Dos Passos but aiming implicitly at all the intellectuals who rose to attack the CP, Gold reached the conclusion: "Intellectuals are the most unstable and untrustworthy group in modern society, one often is forced to believe."[4] Several months later Dos Passos irrefutably confirmed his rejection of Communism in a frank letter to John Howard Lawson. He wrote: "I have come to believe that the CP is fundamentally opposed to our democracy as I see it and that Marxism if held as a dogma, is a reactionary force and an impediment to progress."[5]

There was no independent Communist voice within the popular front to respond to Dos Passos's literary anti-Communism. Granville Hicks as late as spring 1938 in a review of the *U.S.A.* trilogy and *Journeys between Wars* (1938) lamented his move away from the CP while recognizing Dos Passos's importance as an artist. Of course, with the publication in 1939 of his overtly anti-Communist novel depicting the failures of the Party in Spain *(Adventures of a Young Man),* criticism mounted.[6]

The contours of the topography of the cultural front after 1935 were reviewed in chapters 4 and 5. What remains to be done is to see how the central elements of the proletarian phase were carried over and remolded in the development of the popular front. This involves the investigation of three areas: (1) the role of the Party in its work with writers and intellectuals under anti-fascist politics; (2) the acceptance of people's (or progressive) literature as part of the non-revolutionary politics of the popular front; and (3) the full development of the idea of a mass audience, which had its roots at the opening of the decade in the Kharkov Conference.

The clearest statement on the relationship between writers and intellectuals and the Party under the united front comes in Mike Gold's contribution to the Twenty-fifth Anniversary issue of the *New Masses*—an essay entitled "Migratory Intellectuals." The essay is particularly signifi-

cant because it was published in the transition period between the prole-
tarian First Writers' Congress (April, 1935) and the popular front Second
Congress. The essay is a good gauge to the direction of the Party emphasis
in the latter half of the decade: Gold, while speaking to the issue of the
Party as leader of the fight against reaction, is primarily attacking
Trotskyist intellectuals.

Although only Sidney Hook and James T. Farrell are the main antago-
nists in the essay, he is obviously speaking to all those intellectuals once
drawn close to the Party who have moved away and now devote their
energy to attacks on the Party and to the most strident red-baiting. Perhaps
other names should be named: Max Eastman, Charles Yale Harrison, James
Rorty, Edmund Wilson, Louis Hacker, Eugene Lyons, John Dewey, John
Chamberlain. Gold holds them in contempt for believing egotistically that
they know more about what the program for Communism ought to be
than the leaders who really practice Communism: Browder, Foster,
Hathaway, and Dunne. Furthermore, Gold rejects their pompous vanity
and constant harping on theory. They offer, he argues, nothing constructive and form small isolated parties and groups whose primary function is
to ". . .loathe and hate Communist parties of the world more intensely
than they do capitalism. . . ."[7]

At the end of his attack he offers this solution: "If one believes in
Communism, one must also accept the only instrument history has taught
us can bring it—the Communist Party—the two cannot be separated. And
if one chooses the Communist Party . . . one must loyally accept its
decisions—otherwise the party dissolves into chaotic particles."[8] Gold
maintains that the Party consistently supported the working class. And
he explains that the *New Masses* keeps in line with the CP because the
Party "was right more often than any other." Under the line of the united
front Gold points to the success of France and Spain to argue for its
support as the best way to defeat fascism. He ends by pointing an accusing
finger at these same intellectuals, whom he sees sabotaging the people's
struggle against fascism.

While this Bolshevik idea of the unity of theory and practice and of
intelligentsia and worker through the work of a vanguard Party is fine,
the reality in the popular front as we have seen was the virtual absence of a
Communist position that should have been the basis for such work. The
Writers' Congresses became progressively more liberal. The Communist
fractions inside the labor unions were eliminated. There was little in
Communist practice in this period to distinguish it from liberal supporters.
The victory of the working class in terms of the popular front was the
establishment of the C.I.O., the building of the civil liberties, popular
reform, and collective security organizations, and the ties to the New Deal.

Nowhere during the popular front is the confusion over Communism and literature more clearly isolated than in Granville Hicks's review of Horace Gregory's anthology *New Letters in America* (1938). The thesis that Hicks offers in this essay is quite simple: "Communist literature ought to be able to reflect the Communist hope. . . ." Hicks argues that there is no Party line in literature, that there is no dictatorship, and that what the Party offers is hope. The optimism which Hicks preaches is based on the axiom that "Communism is good news." Where a few years before, during the proletarian phase, there had been some efforts at direction, definition, and purpose, Hicks now offers an aesthetic which says simply that a classless society is possible and will come eventually. There is no short-cut to socialism, but the Communists offer hope. His rather harsh review of the younger writers whom Gregory collected is a response to the despair and decay reflected in those writings. He wants to see in literature the "substance of the Communist hope." And so Hicks is waiting "for the author who will show in literature what we know that means in life"—i.e., "Communism is good news."[9]

Hick's gradualism and Gold's belief in the correctness of the Party reflect on the literary front the general notion of a people's party and progress. The Party became, in popular front theory, part of the leadership of the progressive forces. Leadership becomes, in my view, too passive in these terms, i. e., merely to expose and fight fascism and imperialism. As in all "mass work" during the popular front, the Party, hoping to end its sectarian stance, began to change its left Communist line (the call for socialist revolution) in favor of the broader, more unifying themes of anti-fascism and labor union solidarity. People's literature became a substitute for proletarian literature.

Viewing the literary production of the 1930s from late in the popular front, Party literary critics and commentators point to a body of writing which has legitimized, in their view, socially conscious art. As one critic, Arnold Shukotoff, noted in his analysis of the rise of the proletarian short story in the decade, the authors "have developed a pronounced concern with the experiences of the underprivileged and the impact of social forces upon people." He sees writers such as Albert Maltz, Richard Wright, and Pietro di Donato leading the new wave of writers who use the short story to describe *"society at critical moments"* in contrast with the heavily psychological and personal writing of the twenties. He labels this new writing "social realism" and claims that it not only involves new thematic directions but also the resolution of technical problems:

. . . first, how to suggest group experience through the presentation of individual experience; second, how to convince skeptical readers that the unbelievable experiences of the underprivileged are real, not fictitious; finally, how to communicate to the reader, in addition to the sense of participating in the *life of fiction,* the desire to understand and participate in the *life of social action.*[10]

One important measure of the new writings' legitimacy and literary force was the first and second place finishes in the O. Henry Memorial Awards for the best short stories of 1938: Albert Maltz won first prize for "The Happiest Man On Earth," the story of an unemployed young man who demands a job that means certain death—as a truck driver delivering explosives. And Richard Wright took second place for his "Fire and Cloud," a story of a successful multi-racial demonstration for relief.

Samuel Sillen, commenting on the success of these stories sees evidence of the "power and propriety of Marxism."[11] Sillen reiterates this theme in his essay "The People, Yes," written as part of the discussion for the Third Writers' Congress (June 1939). Starting with Maxim Gorky's idea that literature is a unifying force in helping people to understand their sufferings and desires, Sillen argues that the "progressive" writers in America are "the welders of the people's unity." They are not divisive. They support the democratic front. He argues that such writers as Steinbeck, Sandburg, and Robert Sherwood have produced some of the best writing of the period, and have fulfilled Gorky's maxim of making people aware of their common experience and aspiration. They are writers, he claims, who have produced "at once great democratic affirmations and notable works of art." This new trend in literature reflects the unity of writers with the common man and takes national symbols away from the right-wingers. Sillen explains:

The people . . . are the heroes of our most gratifying books—of Elliot Paul's *The Stars and Stripes Forever,* of Ruth McKenney's *Industrial Valley,* of Richard Wright's *Uncle Tom's Children,* of Josephine Herbst's trilogy. The people, yes: in Margaret Bourke-White's and Erskine Caldwell's *You Have Seen Their Faces,* in Archibald MacLeish's *Land of the Free.* . . . They have been successful in the measure that they have been faithful to the people.[12]

The clearest definition of proletarian literature in its popular front form came in an essay in the summer of 1938 written by Joshua Kunitz. It is a response to a letter by poet Walter Lowenfels suggesting that the term "proletarian literature" no longer be used and be replaced instead by "people's literature." Kunitz presented his analysis in the form of an answer to this question: "Does the term 'proletarian literature'—which posits the existence in this country of a proletariat, a proletarian attitude, and proletarian writers to express the attitude—describe a real phenomenon, or is it merely the product of the wishful thinking of a few leftist doctrinaires?"[13] He argues that "proletarian literature" is a term adopted to help describe, measure, and organize an actual phenomenon; it is a useful tool and label.

Kunitz asks Lowenfels to see proletarian literature as "the expression of the proletarian vanguard in the cultural front." Proletarian literature reflects the leading position of the working class in the popular front, he argues. Other terms such as "people's," "progressive," or "democratic" literature are useful because they are broad and inclusive and represent "the literary analogue of the people's front or democratic front." [14] Kunitz's distinction is fuzzy. It suggests the retention of the more specific label because it represents a victory for the working class while at the same time wanting a broader label to correspond in literary terms to the kind of popular front unity demonstrated by the LAW. Unfortunately, this distinction is based on the idea that the working class participates in the democratic front as the revolutionary class and that proletarian literature is a term that has won literary acceptance in an ideological battle and therefore is evidence of a revolutionary conquest. But this revolutionary rhetoric no longer reflected the Party practice.[15]

Virtually every discussion on the importance and defense of proletarian or people's literature was in part an attack on the renegade and Trotskyist intellectuals. An example of this duality is Mike Gold's essay "Notes on the Cultural Front" published late in 1937. Gold is responding to a concerted attack by disaffected intellectuals on the left who offer the thesis that the Party killed proletarian literature (he is obviously responding to Philip Rahv, William Phillips, and James T. Farrell). The evidence for this attack on the Party is the lull in production of proletarian literature since the publication of *Proletarian Literature in the United States: An Anthology* (1935). Gold devotes the first half of the essay to vilifying the Trotskyists' pessimistic attacks on the popular front and the Communist Party.[16]

In the second part of the essay he acknowledges that there has been a lull as writers have come to understand the momentous changes in American political life at a time when the working class organizes in the C.I.O. for a fight, "not only for bread, but for political power." The proletarian movement produced great new spokesmen in such writers as Jack Conroy, Grace Lumpkin, Fielding Burke, Leane Zugsmith, Erskine Caldwell, Albert Maltz, John Spivak, Edwin Rolfe, and Langston Hughes. And Gold expects that they will come to understand the popular front. What had changed? Gold argues that proletarian literature is not dead; rather, one period has ended but a new era of proletarian literature has not yet begun. There are new intellectuals who have, according to Gold, been proletarianized during the depression and are now rooted in mass organizations or trade unions; ultimately these people will reflect the new political reality and create the preconditions for socialism: "These masses of members in the Newspaper Guild, the Lawyers' Guild, and the trade unions of the social workers, architects, and technicians, the teachers, actors, and musicians, authors, and the rest, are new species of 'intellectuals.' They are dwelling in no ivory tower, but in the real world, where ideas must mirror objective truth."[17]

This experience will tie them to the working class and will, in his belief, lead to a new, more complex proletarian literature emerging from the new labor movement—i.e., the C.I.O. The new proletarian literature will reflect the optimism of the success of the popular front, in spite of the attacks of the Trotskyists. For Gold the early proletarian literature "carved a road despite the Menckens and Cabells and Max Eastmans of yesterday. It will go on widening the road despite the new crop of ivory-tower Iagos, Communist-haters and naysayers to life."[18]

It is clear that the conversion was made. Proletarian, people's, or progressive literature became the revolutionary expression on the literary front during the last four years of the decade. The Party became the defender and propagandizer of socially conscious art and rationalized this with the rhetorical notions of revolution by making the tacit assumption that attachment to the working class or the masses and support for the mass struggles meant a direct tie to the Party. Sadly, it was a connection more metaphysical than real.

Last, we come to the issue of audience. It is one area of remarkable consistency throughout the decade. The reason is obvious enough: the more readers one brought to the Party or Marxism, the more influence one had. Much of the discussion over audience involved playing with numbers to "objectively" demonstrate that influence. Clearly, the Party wanted to expand the audience for its own press and for proletarian literature and for people's art. This is reflected in the circulation drives of the *New Masses* and *DW,* the opening of book stores, and the creating of book clubs. It is reflected in the critical reviews in all areas of culture.

A serious and comprehensive attempt to analyze the publishing field appears at the end of the popular front and directly reveals all the concerns over audience expressed throughout the decade and speaks, also, to political and literary concerns.

The article "The Fight for Popular-Priced Books," written by Samuel Sillen and Milton Meltzer, argues for less expensive editions of important books—i.e., books for the masses at reasonable cost. The article was triggered by the publication in late autumn of 1938 of a two-volume collection of Lincoln Steffen's letters—Granville Hicks and Ella Winter (Steffens's wife), editors, *The Letters of Lincoln Steffens.* The set was priced at ten dollars.

In an extensive piece of research Sillen and Meltzer analyze readership, the economics of the publishing industry, and the needs of authors. Given the dominant ideology of the popular front, their conclusions are fascinating. Though they recognize that price is the basic problem, they suggest that there really is little antagonism between the reader, author, and publisher. They are "concerned with an inquiry into the realistic possibilities, within the framework of the profit system, of a wider distribution of books." Also they are convinced that "the strengthening of our democracy depends in large part on a much wider distribution of good books."[19]

Their basic thesis is that the publishing industry should commence the distribution of lower cost editions and should try for higher volume. But the politics and aesthetics of this call are worth noting. They write:

The progressive movement has a lot to gain from the widening of the book audience in America. The radio, newspapers, magazines, and movies, media controlled by big business, mislead public opinion more often than they inform it. It is hard for an author of progressive views to find a publisher among those who issue expensive books for a limited audience. But when book prices are brought within reach of an audience of millions, the problem changes. The publisher must select authors whose work will appeal to these millions. The experience of low cost book publishers shows that great numbers of people want progressive books. . . .[20]

The class struggle has evaporated. The publishers who want profit will make it from huge sales of popular literature. The progressive writers will have their messages read by the masses. And in some vague way the political consciousness of the nation will be changed. The submergence of Communist politics leads irrevocably to liberal optimism, but not to socialism.

PART 3

MARXIST
AESTHETIC THEORY

CHAPTER 9

AN ANALYSIS

The methodology suggested by the preceding analysis of the CPUSA and its Soviet antecedents in the 1930s argues that a Marxist view of aesthetics must be tied to the specific work of an active Communist Party and that Marxist aesthetics is fundamentally political, not artistic. The focus must be on the Communist Party as it develops a political line and program. However, most Marxist analyses dealing with culture are directed at finding a grand aesthetic formula with which to evaluate literature and art. I believe that such formulas cannot be successfully developed, and when attempted in this way contradict the substance of historical materialism as the basic method of Marxist inquiry.

This chapter does not attempt a comprehensive overview and analysis of extant material on Marxist aesthetics. Such a review would be a study in itself.[1] The intent here is to evaluate three basic tendencies in Marxist aesthetic theorizing, showing their inherent weaknesses and my methodological differences with them. The tendencies are: (1) the attempt to isolate the scattered "dicta" of Marx and Engels and to convert them into a complete theory of aesthetics; (2) the attempt to show the connection between economic base and aspects of the superstructure (literature or culture, for example); and (3) the attempt to interpret art in sociological, ideological, or dialectical contexts.

The examples for each of these tendencies have been selected carefully to highlight the major issues and to contrast sharply with my own study. The first section of this chapter evaluates the "dicta" of Marx and Engels edited by Lee Baxandall and Stefan Morawski, two well-respected Marxist critics.[2] Their critical analysis is, I believe, the *most recent* significant effort to convert the writings, comments, and letters of Marx and Engels into a coherent aesthetics.

In the second section I analyze the aesthetic theories of George Plekhanov, a distinguished early Russian Marxist and an important historical figure, whose work on aesthetics offers an explanation of the connection between art and the superstructure.

The third section is a review of a variety of very well-known and scholarly critics who treat the issues of sociology, ideology, and dialectics in relation to art. Included are Ernst Fischer, Arnold Hauser, Lucien Goldmann, and Frederick Jameson.

Although there are significant differences between each broad tendency and the next (and obviously differences among the individual critics), there are several points of correspondence uniting all of this material: in each case considered here there is the attempt to take the specific research and generalize it into a universal Marxist aesthetic formula, claiming that the formula is derived from an analysis based on the method of "historical materialism." Their approaches apply "historical materialism" as a short-cut. They fail to understand that it is a method of inquiry, and that this method is a guide to asking the right questions, rather than in itself a set of answers.

This approach is expressed in the deification of the "masters" of Marxism or inconsistent application of the method of historical materialism, either of which results in the spinning of mechanical formulas.[3] The aesthetics which emerges from these writers is, as I see it, abstract and impractical, based on complex theoretical equations and imprecise definitions.

The three basic tendencies mentioned above have a common origin in a series of now very famous comments by Marx and Engels. Most important perhaps is the comment in Marx's preface to *A Contribution to the Critique of Political Economy* suggesting that the material basis of life determines the intellectual processes.[4] Marx intimates that the economic base is the significant factor which, if understood, may provide an explanation for culture and aesthetics. The temptation in the literature is to try to articulate an interpretive method which makes that jump—from economics to aesthetics—as if there were a linear connection. Furthermore, one is prompted to ask where one must look to find the source of these aesthetic ideas located in the superstructure if they are in fact connected to an economic base. Marx and Engels seem to provide the major answer in another famous quotation from *The German Ideology:* "The ideas of the ruling class are in every epoch the ruling ideas; i.e., the class, which is the ruling material force. . . ."[5] And intellectual achievement is connected to the class nature of the society. The temptation here is to argue the primacy of class analysis in the understanding of literature and to open the problems of consciousness, ideology, and "false consciousness."[6]

The critics discussed below have taken these brief asides by Marx and Engels and from them have articulated several striking and provocative questions about art and its role in society. For example: (1) If a materialist conception assumes that history is made by the actions of men in the "real" world but also that these actions are often at cross-purposes and undertaken with false consciousness, how then can one arrive at true understanding of some component of that world—e.g., art works? (2) What are the primary considerations in studying a particular art work—its historical development, an analysis of form and content, a biography of its creator? (3) What details, contradictions, or connections about the art work or its creator are worth knowing?

Although such questions are fascinating and important, the critics studied here have not connected their aesthetics to the real work of Communists. They make no connection of theory to practice. They seem to be searching for a major formula with which to answer questions about the social relationships of men. In my view, dialectical materialism is a tool to be applied to these relations and their history. For me the answer is a rigorous historical study evaluating the specific activities of Communists as they integrate artistic issues into their political work. From this perspective I undertake the criticism of their work.

1

Of special importance in the Baxandall and Morawski collection is the long introductory essay contributed by Morawski in which he argues that the writings of Marx and Engels on literature and art can be synthesized into a coherent aesthetic theory. The intent is to prove through his (and Baxandall's) new ordering and analysis that this work of Marx and Engels must be interpreted as the basis for Marxist aesthetics:

. . .to suggest that Marx and Engels provided a rounded, balanced aesthetic theory would be incorrect. On the other hand, to dismiss their ideas as fortuitous or incidental speculations, or as utterances of mere taste and preference, would be just as irresponsible. . . . The [aesthetic] ideas are addressed to problems that are thought to rank among the most significant and fundamental according to all traditional aesthetic treatises up to today.

. . . .

The body of the aesthetic thought of Marx and Engels is not all-encompassing, and ostensibly it centers on literary examples. No final or complete system is offered. However, the contribution which an aesthetic approach makes eludes definition by such a test. A proper standard would be the originality of the contribution . . . and its influence . . . . By this test, the aesthetic ideas of Marx and Engels have historical and theoretical importance.[7]

Before criticizing the arguments and evidence with which Morawski supports these conclusions, it is important to note the central questions which this approach to Marxist aesthetics uncovers. To suggest that the writings of Marx and Engels on art and literature provide a coherent theory and that therefore their writings are the proper starting point is not as simple and direct as it appears. There is considerable difficulty in merely pointing to appropriate segments of their writings. First, they did not specifically analyze the problem of aesthetics or its relation to literature. There is no definitive study nor even a preliminary comment since Marx and Engels never consciously attempted a systematic approach to this issue. What exists are philosophical statements containing basic assumptions, analyses of particular historical and economic problems, and letters containing both direct and indirect comments pertaining to aesthetics. Second, the crucial issue becomes the approach toward this so-called primary material. Why begin with their "offhand" remarks? Does one merely extend offhand remarks into formulations of aesthetics? Does one attempt to organize the scattered comments into a coherent aesthetic theory and then label it the aesthetics of Marx and Engels, as if they consciously produced it? Furthermore, to juxtapose in some manner quotations from several decades and contexts into a theory is a crude technique that must be clearly marked as ahistorical.

It will be shown that the central weakness of the Morawski analysis is the failure to create a usable aesthetics once the clarification of Marx and Engels is complete. Essentially, he tries to clarify the writings of Marx and Engels and to integrate his new approach with the previous scholarship. His synthesis becomes part of the academic debate over the *correct* interpretation. Basically, his arguments hinge on intellectual pedantry (the search for aesthetic motifs in their work) and suggestive prophecy (how sensibility and creativity will change in a classless society).[8] Despite Morawski's seemingly objective approach in trying to tie together the wide variety of comments of Marx and Engels into a coherent whole and his erudite and sophisticated framework, he does not transcend the intellectual and academic debate.

The essay does present a review of previous scholarship which attempted to synthesize the work of Marx and Engels into a coherent aesthetic, but *it is primarily designed to argue that their comments do provide the necessary framework for a Marxist aesthetic.* He orders the essay under these topic headings: (1) A Note on the Texts and Previous Interpretations; (2) The Preliminary Problems; (3) General Methodological Assumptions and Dominant Themes; (4) The Chief Aesthetic Problems Considered by Marx and Engels, and (5) Background to the Aesthetic Thought of Marx and Engels.[9]

Morawski's synthesis begins in part two, "The Preliminary Problems:" ". . . by (a) discussing whether two phases, one pre-Marxian and the other Marxian, appear in their writings on art and literature and by (b) outlining the thematic pattern of structural coherences to be found among their many scattered ideas and comments."[10] The vision of unity which Morawski wishes to impose sees Marx and Engels as inheritors of both Hegel and Feuerbach but also as men who then push on to develop their own distinctive world view. Morawski's belief is that Marx and Engels are both humanists and revolutionaries. He organizes the available material from Marx and Engels on three levels: (1) dominant themes—a developed topic; (2) observations—a thesis but no development; and (3) remarks.

In the first category are to be found most of the issues providing the topic headings in the selection of texts; i.e., the origin of aesthetic sensibility, the alienation which affects the artist and his work, the problem of realism, "tendency" writing, the class equivalents of art. . . . Among the semi-finished themes of the second category, we find: the distinguishing traits of aesthetic objects and aesthetic experience; the recurrent attributes and enduring values of art; the comic and the tragic; form and style. The third category, comprised of brief comments, includes topics such as the distinction between science and art, the role of philosophy in artistic creation, and the hierarchy of artistic values.[11]

The purpose of this section is twofold: First, it allows Morawski to comment on the debate over early and late Marx—namely, where to place the *Economic and Philosophic Manuscripts of 1844*.[12] His view is that a unity exists between Hegel and Marx and a consistency exists within the entirety of Marx's writings. Second, it provides Morawski with the opportunity which conforms to his general plan to stress the humanist aspect of Marx and Engels, showing them to be part of an aesthetic tradition in Western culture and not critics who break from it.

Part three, "General Methodological Assumptions and Dominant Themes," develops this latter point in the context of his own interpretation of the underlying hypotheses of Marxism. This discussion begins with an assertion that, despite many disagreements on the general question of Marxist aesthetics, there is consensus on one point:

Aesthetic phenomena are studied in a context of socio-historical processes, and in this way are regarded as part of a broad, "civilizational" activity by which the species *homo sapiens* advances slowly to realize an innate potential. Art objects are not isolated phenomena, but are mutually dependent with other cultural activity of predominantly social, political, moral, religious, or scientific character.[13]

This assertion is supported by an abstract analysis incorporating philosophical terms as "synchronic," "diachronic," "idiogenetic," "allogenetic," etc., leading to a conclusion that the structure of Marxist aesthetic thought is historicist: "These elements of mutuality in a context and of a dynamics of change cohere into a methodological position when one seeks to approach the various problems posed by aesthetic objects and aesthetic activity. The best name for the approach is *historicism.*" [14] Although this forceful proposition suggests that the dominant themes on the origin of art and its function can be understood only on the basis of historical data, the historical analysis which he provides is insufficient. The connection between dominant themes and history is this: one should consider *the genesis of art* within the context of the historical activity of all homo sapiens—which he suggests is the ongoing struggle to become free;however, this struggle for freedom is trapped within the context of class societies. Phenomena such as art must have *class equivalents,* and this class nature leads to *alienation.* Furthermore, his historical approach does not deny a certain autonomy to aesthetic ideas and artistic expressions: ". . . *realism* is common in art and literature; so is the evidence of the artist's socio-political *'tendency,'*" which in turn are manifestations of the historical process and "its ideological patterns." Finally, he suggests that an analysis of these terms, "realism" and "tendency," will also lead to their corollaries: the importance of human labor in creating culture, of social revolution as unavoidable and desirable, and of Communist commitment as an ideal which humanity adopts as a means of advancing change. [15]

A precise interpretation of Morawski on this issue is difficult, given the level of abstraction. It seems that there is a governing historical methodology through which one should come to understand the dominant aesthetic themes. His historical view extends over the entire development of the *species.* The developing pattern which he accepts is evolutionary—from precapitalist to capitalist to socialist society. The end is a socialist society that permits social appropriation of social production.

In the context of this approach, Morawski argues that art is a special category requiring unique treatment; he suggests that Marx accepts this notion of uniqueness and that it is in fact a carryover from Hegel. [16] The evidence for this interpretation is developed in the fourth part of the essay, "The Chief Aesthetic Problems Considered by Marx and Engels." This section of his essay is devoted to a discussion of six major areas of concern from which dominant themes emerge. [17]

First, on the origin of aesthetic sensibility, Morawski argues that "Marx explained aesthetic sensibility as very gradually taking shape among the specific formations of concrete historical processes—foremostly as part of the development of human labor." Here is the outline of the path of development of aesthetic sensibility which he claims can be attributed to Marx through his writings:

(a) At first, art developed; it was a kind of bonus as primitive workers formed objects . . . and expressed their powers to master the material world.
(b) After much time, the structure of the object (its inherent *Mass*, measure, proportion) could come to chiefly occupy the artisan's attention. At this stage, obsessive functionalism started to fade, and a practical aesthetic contemplation could begin to emerge.
(c) Aesthetic responsiveness to "given" physical attributes such as color, timbre, etc., could develop at a later time. . . .

Morawski makes several judgments based on these propositions: the origin of aesthetic sensibility fits well into Marx's general ideas about the way in which humanity molds the material world; aesthetic experience is a mixture of intellectual, emotional, and sensual activities which conveniently allows one to integrate mimesis and intuition, ideology and "apractical" (sic) art, autotelicism and connectedness with other human activity; and finally, Marx's theory is basically a *Gehaltasthetik*—a content-oriented aesthetic.[18]

Second, on alienation, Morawski argues this proposition:

Progress beyond the animal status was the cost of engendering oppression, exploitation, and character disorder. Through this rigorous and inexorable civilizational dynamic, aesthetic activity and art objects were both developed and forced into patterns partially thwarting their potential realization.
Yet, if alienation has been inseparable from aesthetic phenomena in all historical eras, it undoubtedly became more intensive, in Marx's judgment, as the market conditions of capitalism developed. The capitalist market transformed art into a commodity, which it had never been before.

Morawski's perception is that this notion of alienation is readily applicable to artists. (And he also suggests that there is a countervailing process occurring—called disalienation. Disalienation is the movement toward Communism which he believes would also directly affect both workers and artists.) Without succumbing to pure prophecy or simplistic utopianism, he makes this summary:

Not attempting any detailed prediction, Marx mentioned three elements regarding this expectation:
1. The creative abilities of individuals would be fully developed. . . .
2. The character of work would become increasingly aesthetic. . . .
3. Every person would grow capable of artistic achievement in every domain of the arts. . . .[19]

Third, on class values embodied in art, he argues the importance of connecting this theme with the issue of alienation: "Whatever the class or social values held and manifested by the artist, their motivation or cause will lie in the alienation which afflicts art and social life." Morawski suggests two possible interpretations:

> . . . either of two Marxian emphases can be given to interpretation of the class conditioning of artistic values. In the more deterministic sense this notion means that the expression of the work of art will conform to the ideology of a particular class, as imposed upon and mediated by the artist. A more comprehensive interpretation will find that the class conditioning . . . primarily occurs . . . where epochal class conflicts are depicted with lucid and deft control by artists who have an exceptional awareness of the historical framework and the dynamic of the tale they would tell.[20]

It is this latter approach which Morawski prefers and sees as more adequate because it leads directly to the next (fourth) area of interest, realism.

On the issue of realism, he argues that the term signifies a "typifying" social representation, not a comment on formal structure or on the origins of art. He states: ". . . realism can be described as the artistic-cognitive value of an artwork. . . . Authenticity of realism was to be achieved by, and judged by, the expression of a cognitive equivalent: specifically, the dominant and typical traits of socially conflicted life in a particular place and time."

Fifth, on the issue of "tendency" writing (tendentiousness), Morawski argues that Marx and Engels define it as the acceptance of a politicized art incorporating a historical world view compatible with their belief in the eventual development of a socialist society. Here is the definition which he provides: ". . . 'tendency' writing, the projection by essentially discursive yet poeticized means of an idea of history and of the attitudes, feelings, conflicts, etc., of the artistic personality (the author) about this idea."[21]

And finally, on the problem of expression of fundamental human values in art, Morawski, citing the praise for Greek art, argues for this judgment: "Because 'form' was less important to them than 'content' and in light of Marx's unwavering attachment to the Greek example and to the ideal of disalienated humanity . . . the top priority among the enduring values, for Marx and Engels, should be recognized as the fundamentally human value embodied in art."[22]

Despite his often convoluted and abstract analysis of these six major areas, Morawski has managed to provide a coherent schema to the scattered writings. But it is a coherence supplied by a hypothesis that is suspect. Morawski proceeds from the assumption that art is sui generis and that Marx and Engels recognized and accepted it as such. This assertion is not fully revealed until the final subsection of part four—on the problem of expression of fundamental human values in art. He states that the primary aesthetic issues are problems of form, originality, and style—things with which a Marxist aesthetic must necessarily deal. He *asserts* that Marx and Engels were very sensitive to these aspects of aesthetics despite their emphasis on content. (He does acknowledge that there is little if any written evidence to support this claim.)

Why then does he choose this approach? It seems that this interpretation of their writings on art and literature functions as a means of incorporating Marxism into the general development of aesthetics in Western culture, of pronouncing it a fit academic discipline, and of permitting the inclusion of the broadest range of critics under the rubric of Marxism.[23] This approach also fits well into Morawski's vision of the significance of the humanist interpretation of Marx and Engels. His view suggests that Marx and Engels believed art objects to be very special phenomena with inherent distinctive traits, and a theme of uniqueness filters into Morawski's analysis of several of the dominant themes. For example, he argues that despite their hard-line view of the class nature of society, they mitigated class analysis when discussing literature; they did not admit ideology to a central place in artistic realism; they accepted the notion that autonomy in art is part of our human heritage and that man's early freedom is possible once again in a socialist society. In essence, his interpretation of the dominant themes is the view that art has a special, unpractical, and autonomous role.[24]

In part five, "Background to the Aesthetic Thought of Marx and Engels," Morawski catalogs the background sources, analyzes previous attempts at organizing the aesthetics of Marx and Engels, and assesses the position of his (and Baxandall's) work. He calls for an empirical, complete, and systematic study of the intellectual background to their aesthetic thought, what he labels as the idiogenetic sources. Morawski believes that Marx and Engels fit into the general pattern of development of Western culture. He states that "German classical aesthetics may be considered the primary source of their aesthetic thought." (Not Hegel alone!) He also suggests that as erudite scholars Marx and Engels must have been familiar with other current thinkers such as Rousseau and the French utopian socialists. He argues that there is a tradition of non-aesthetic thought that must be noted: for example, Hegel's general philosophy; the new historicist perspective (Vico, Montesquieu, Winckelmann, and Herder); English economists; French historians. He also believes that despite their attack on Romanticism, one must acknowledge that they were "cradled by Romanticism."

This has been the catalogue of what Marx and Engels accepted from their background and critically assimilated into their intellectual system. What they rejected is also important. . . . Directly or indirectly, Marx and

Engels attacked the objective idealism of Krause, Weisse, and Hegel, and the subjective idealism of Kant, Fichte, the *romantische Schule*. They rejected the art for art's sake doctrine, and equally, or nearly so, they opposed a banal didacticism. While respecting the value of form, they opposed formalism. They did not disclaim the presence of a natural impulsion underlying aesthetic experience, but they did not agree with the naturalist notion that a specific aesthetic instinct was common both to man and other animals.[25]

The method by which one understands the aesthetics of Marx and Engels, according to Morawski, is to root their ideas in the Western cultural tradition and to suggest that their primary value is the freshness of their interpretation.

The intellectual position of Marx and Engels is further explored in his analysis of previous attempts to synthesize and order their writings on art and literature.[26] Morawski sees three basic errors in the previous approaches to the issues of the aesthetic thoughts of Marx and Engels. The first basic error is typified by Mikhail Lifshitz, who fails, according to Morawski, to account for the influence of the history of aesthetics on Marx and Engels, ". . . that is to say, the idiogenetic sources of their aesthetic thought." Despite this criticism, there is much in Lifshitz that Morawski accepts, though in less polemical terms. Morawski aligns with Lifshitz on these points: (1) that Marx continues in his post-1844 work to comment on art—e.g., in *Critique of Political Economy;* (2) that Marx rejects superficial comparisons between intellectual and material production (a notion that Morawski stresses to help support the contention that art is unique); (3) that Marx viewed the development of art as determined by the dialectical conception of history—i.e., the decline of artistic creativity is a function of the growth of bourgeois society; and (4) that in a class society art and culture inevitably assume a class nature.[27]

The second mistaken approach is that of G. Fridlender, who "takes the dictum from Lenin that Marxism's primary sources are the German classical philosophy, the English political economy, and the French utopian socialism, and applies this schema indiscriminately."[28] Fridlender's thesis also argues for a view that a coherent aesthetic can be constructed from the scattered remarks and that one does not have to be overly dogmatic in accepting their dictum on aesthetics—i.e., one should accept their comments in an "historical" context. What Morawski rejects is Fridlender's didacticism, of which the following is a representative example: "Correctly understood, all these utterances as a whole (and each of them individually) are a most important achievement of human thought, an invaluable tool of theoretical and historical research—a tool whose significance has been tested and proved by the practical experience of human history in the last one hundred years."[29]

And third, Morawski rejects the scientific and class connections which Trofimov, who uses both Lifshitz and Fridlender, attempts to build, but accepts his view that Marx and Engels made a significant contribution to aesthetics:

The appearance of the aesthetics of Marxism marked a radical change in the history of aesthetic thought. . . . This radical change, conditioned above all by the same world-historical revolution in philosophy which the founders of Marxism brought about, signals a totally new period of development of aesthetics, which became for the first time an authentic science. . . .

. . . .

Some revisionists insist that Marx and Engels established no aesthetics at all. . . . Naturally, all these assertions are without foundation. The special features of the origin and characteristic points of Marxist philosophy have a direct relationship with Marxist aesthetics, which is dependent upon Marxist philosophy. In addition, the origin and development of Marxist aesthetics are inseparable from the political and economic ideas of the founders of scientific communism.[30]

Before attempting a comprehensive critique of Morawski one last quotation is necessary. In the conclusion to his essay Morawski presents a brief analysis of the *new contributions* made by Marx and Engels:

Marx and Engels contributed to a new understanding of the priorities among values embodied by art. They found a new solution to the old dilemma which saw art at once dying out and providing hope and comfort to a presently suffering humanity. The achievement of *homo aestheticus* could be anticipated, Marx thought, but a radical socio-political change in the situation of the species would be required. . . . Tendentiousness acquires a new meaning in Marx and Engels. . . . *Tendenz* is recast in the context of the Marxian world view, and historical reality itself is described as "tendentious.". . . The Hegelian notion of a type. . . is accepted, but they introduce to realism an awareness of the socially emergent elements. Ideology here comes to be considered a component of artistic choice and discrimination . . . the genesis of aesthetic sensibility is newly interpreted by reference to dialectical and historical materialism. And the transformation of *homo faber* to *homo ludens* is seen as a profoundly social phenomenon. . . . The dominant theme of class equivalents of art, we know, has been accepted universally as a Marxian emphasis; and while the class dimension of art has been observed earlier, Marx and Engels were the first ones to see it in its proper dimension and to explore the complexities . . . the dominant themes of Marx and Engels presented new issues for nineteenth-century aesthetics.[31]

The intent of this lengthy overview of Morawski is to show that one cannot proceed to develop fundamentals of a Marxist aesthetics without clearly articulated guiding principles—which begins, I believe, by making judgments about what one believes Marxism to be. In this particular case, Morawski provides no rationalization for trying to structure an aesthetic out of the writings of Marx and Engels. The supposition must be that in building, glueing, extrapolating, and recreating their thoughts into a coherent statement on aesthetics, one has established the foundation of Marxist aesthetics—or at a minimum *a* Marxist aesthetic. He chooses not to explain why one should seek an aesthetic in their writings or even why one should begin with their comments.

However, the problem which persists and nags in the Morawski essay is simply this: Why does an analysis which begins with Marx and Engels and is rooted in their "general" philosophical orientation become automatically Marxist? Marx and Engels offer no dialectical materialist analysis of literature, art, or culture. Clearly, they were often interested in aesthetic issues, which is not unusual considering their intellectual training and background and the variety of writers whom they knew. But why confuse their scattered comments and opinions with what they call the method of "dialectical materialism"—a methodology rooted in what they considered concrete historical fact and scientific objectivity and precision? Not all the opinions of Marx and Engels are "Marxist." They were not messiahs or prophets who alone held magical formulas. They struggled against just such mechanical responses.

Compounding this weakness is his failure to suggest, after developing such a complex and sophisticated analysis and selection of documents, *a usable aesthetic*. Although he succinctly states what he considers to be the original contributions of Marx and Engels to aesthetics, his aesthetic system is so broad, in fact, that it simply becomes part of the Humanist intellectual tradition reaching back to the Enlightenment and winding through the British empiricists, and Kant and other Germans. It is more intellectual history than an evocation of an aesthetic.

Furthermore, even as Morawski presents it, the coherence of Marx and Engels to their "idiogenetic" context does not provide on any level (historical, dialectical, or class) a tool with which to treat literature or art. Instead, Morawski has presented an imprecise set of intellectual constructs that suggests Marxist aesthetics is as respectable as other aesthetics. This is, in fact, his justification for analyzing the origins of their ideas and his belief that a Marxist aesthetic can and should be based on their original comments.

His extensive research into Marx and Engels gives added academic respectability to their thoughts and to the notion that these men provide a valuable source of "fresh" ideas which deserve to be considered. However, Morawski really does no more than deepen the debate over the issue of correct interpretation. The final judgment must be that studying the writings of Marx and Engels *does not* make for Marxism unless one chooses, as he has done, to define it that way.

2

Many of the early propagators of Marxism had comments and suggestions about aesthetic issues, but perhaps the most influential thinker has been George Plekhanov (1856-1918) in terms of both theory and practical effects. His significance and the reasons for inclusion here may be summarized: (1) Plekhanov's work on the problem of aesthetics is often cited as *elemental;* it is an attempt to make a direct connection between art and society based on a "materialist" approach;[32] (2) he considered aesthetic questions to be a primary area for analysis by Marxists, believing that a serious and consistent effort was required to expound a Marxist interpretation of art and literature; (3) he represents, very clearly, an attempt to convert one aspect of the dictum of Marx and Engels (the relationship of base to superstructure) into a system of aesthetic analysis (and much of the difficulty with his work on aesthetics arises, as in the work of Marx and Engels, from the larger philosophical and ideological assumptions).

Plekhanov's wide-ranging writings on historical materialism, culture, and literature connected to his active participation in political work make him a particularly interesting and worthwhile representative of elemental interpreters and extenders of Marx and Engels. But more importantly, it is his emphasis on systematizing the study of art and culture and on connecting it to social characteristics that makes him a necessary component of this general theoretical overview. His work is the basis for much of Marxist thinking on the social foundations of art. He is most often cited as the originator of the sociological interpretation of art from a Marxist perspective.

Among Marxists he was the first to discuss art and literature systematically. He dealt with entire periods of national cultures as often as he wrote on single works, figures, and problems. His knowledge and sensibility were capacious. His findings were arrived at in conscious reference to the German idealist and romantic aestheticians, among them Kant, Hegel, and Schiller—whom, as Marx said of his revisions of Hegel, Plekhanov sought to "stand on their feet." At the same time Plekhanov was productive in philosophy and political theory; he promulgated and headed the Russian revolutionary movement for many years and was Lenin's valued preceptor, although their views came to differ in many respects. No pre-1917 Marxist was so articulate as he on the elements of aesthetic judgment. Marx and Engels to be sure provided the initial and essential impetus; but Marx never wrote the book he planned on Balzac, nor did he complete his encyclopedia article on aesthetics. He and Engels . . . left only opinions on questions of art in letters, in paragraphs in works on other topics, and in tangential references. Contemporaries of Plekhanov such as Franz Mehring, Paul Lafargue, Clara Zetkin, William Liebknecht, Rosa Luxemburg, Leon Trotsky and Anatoli Lunacharsky wrote also on problems of art but without his amplitude and seldom with his rigor.[33]

Plekhanov's major statements on the relationship of art and society are incorporated into two collections of essays: *Art and Social Life* and *Art and Society.*[34] In these essays he attempts to show that art is a social phenomenon best understood through an explanation provided by the "materialist conception of history." Plekhanov believes that this approach to art proves three basic tenets: (1) labor precedes art; (2) art is social; and (3) art reflects class struggle. In his "Letters without Address" he argues:

. . . I am firmly convinced that we shall understand precisely nothing of the history of primitive art unless we become imbued with the idea that labour is older than art and that in general man first looks on objects and phenomena from a utilitarian point of view and only afterwards takes up an aesthetic attitude in his relationship to them.
. . . there can be no doubt that art acquires a social significance only in so far as it depicts, evokes or conveys *actions, emotions and events that are of significance to society.*[35]

In his essay on French drama and painting in the eighteenth century, he develops a synthesis between his view of the genesis of artistic work in the social life and his view of the influence of class structure. He argues that there is a direct and observable correspondence between art (including the work itself, its acceptance by the audience, and its critical reception) and the means of production. Essentially, he states that changes in art, both in form and content, are determined by class struggle.[36]

The materialist core of his analysis suggests a rather simple dichotomy or contradiction observable when analyzing art in a social context: Art is either progressive or unprogressive. Either "art must further the development of human consciousness and contribute to the improvement of the social order or art is an *end in itself,* and to convert it into a means for achieving extraneous ends, no matter how noble, results in a lessening of its dignity."[37] For Plekhanov, two essential questions arise in relation to this dichotomy: (1) In what social context do "art for art's sake" tendencies arise? and (2) Under what social conditions does the "utilitarian" attitude toward art arise?

Starting from his analysis of French literature, he concludes that "the tendency toward art for art's sake arises when discord exists between the artist and his social movement."[38] He ties this directly to the class struggle between the dominant bourgeoisie and the rising proletariat. His judgment is that the artist tied to the bourgeois class presents work which tries to escape reality. Such efforts are manifested in movements like mysticism, formalism, etc.—"isms" represent art for art's sake ideology. He believes that artists who turn away from reality become separated from the community (society) and are thereby separated from the "emancipatory" ideas of the time. And of course, in the end this serves the bourgeois class. He notes: "The reader will recall Leconte de Lisle's remark that poetry gives 'an ideal existence to those with no real life.' And when man loses all spiritual contact with the people among whom he lives, his world of ideas ceases to have any connection with life on earth . . . he turns into a mystic."[39]

It is only utilitarian art, however, which has the possibility of becoming progressive art. Art is progressive when it is connected to a class which can push society forward and when it provides a means of communication among broad segments of the society. For Plekhanov, of course, this class is the proletariat.

The so-called utilitarian concept of art, that is, the tendency to regard the function of art as a judgment on the phenomena of life and a readiness to participate in social struggles, develops and becomes established when a natural bond of sympathy exists between a considerable section of society and those more or less actively interested in artistic creation.[40]

The dichotomy noted above is essentially a function of the class nature of society. For Plekhanov unprogressive art is bourgeois art—an art devoid of content. The attempts of the bourgeoisie to maintain control and dominance over society and all its workings have a deleterious effect on art:

We find, then, under the present social conditions the theory of art for art's sake does not yield very luscious fruits. The extreme individualism of bourgeois decadence shuts artists off from the sources of true inspiration. It sets up a barrier, screening tumultuous social events and condemning them to endless confusion over their petty personal experiences and morbid fantasies. The net result of such ruination is art which not only bears no relation to any kind of beauty—but which is obviously absurd, and justifiable only through a sophistic distortion of the idealist theory of knowledge.[41]

Plekhanov's judgment is based on hypotheses which suggest that ideas have value in direct proportion to their connectedness with progressive and emerging classes: "The ideas of the ruling class lose their intrinsic value at the rate at which that class approaches extinction, and the art created in the spirit of that class decays at the same rate."[42]

The not unexpected conclusion is, of course, that the bourgeoisie is a declining class, that art tied to such a class must necessarily incorporate "fallacious" ideas, and that such art must suffer a decline in aesthetic quality. The explanation is quite linear: artists who defend the bourgeoisie in such a period will find the value and forcefulness of their effort diminished and without inspiration.

The central problem in his theoretical construct is a contradiction arising between what he calls objective (i.e., scientific) and aesthetic (i.e., intuitive) judgments. Plekhanov defines art as a special mode of communication (or as a "communion among men"): "I consider . . . that art begins at the point where man evokes within himself anew feelings and *thoughts* experienced by him under the influence of his environment and *gives a certain expression to them in images*." [43] This he claims is a social phenomenon requiring the critic ". . . to translate the idea of a given work 'from the language of art to the language of sociology'—to find for a work its 'sociological equivalent,' by which Plekhanov meant revealing the class consciousness expressed in a work and the social factors that entered into its creation." [44] And it seems clear enough that Plekhanov has succeeded in showing that art as part of the superstructure does participate in the class struggle, even when it is apparently neutral or escapist—i.e., by serving the interests of the bourgeois class.[45]

Sociological interpretation of art has been accepted as a basic tenet of Marxist aesthetics. However, Plekhanov's approach to criticism is not limited to this single aspect; it has a second and connected premise. The second element requires the critic to determine the aesthetic merit of a work. On the first level it is social objectivism, but on the second it is aesthetic relativism. Plekhanov's approach asks one to accept the notion that art does in fact have a place outside of the class struggle. It has its own law(s) and should be judged both on social and aesthetic terms. (Interestingly, a position very close to Trotsky's.)

Insisting that art is distinctive and that aesthetic sense is non-rational ultimately makes his approach subjective. This does not invalidate the social connections which he uncovers; however, it does dilute the Marxist content.[46] The attempt to create a Marxist aesthetic must, I believe, avoid making art an end in itself. Rather, such an aesthetic must uncover the nature of art, through systematic and historical study, and in turn use that knowledge not to spin grand theories or expound pat formulas but to come to an "objective" understanding of its purpose.

3

The intent of this section is to review representative samples of research that have attempted to amplify and extend the ideas of Marx and Engels on society, ideology, and class, as these ideas pertain to art and aesthetics. Once again the intent is not to present a comprehensive analysis but rather to indicate the variety of studies touching on the relevant themes in Marx and Engels.[47] These studies cover such areas as origins of art, sociology and art, ideology and art, and dialectics and art. The examples were chosen for analysis as samples and as a background against which to judge my approach to the American CP in the 1930s.

On the first of these problems, uncovering the origin of art in the developing of mankind, Ernst Fischer in his *The Necessity of Art: A Marxist Approach* (1963) offers a provocative idea. He sees "magic" as a fundamental source of art, arguing as his thesis that

. . . art in its origins was *magic,* a magic aid towards mastering a real but unexplored world. Religion, science, and art were combined in a latent form . . . in magic. This magic role of art has progressively given way to the role of illuminating social relationships. . . .

True as it is that the essential function of art for a class destined to change the world is not that of *making magic* but of *enlightening* and *stimulating action,* it is equally true that a magic residue in art cannot be entirely eliminated, for without the minute residue of its original nature, art ceases to be art.

. . . .

Art is necessary in order that man should be able to recognize and change the world. But art is also necessary by virtue of the magic inherent in it.[48]

In his first chapter, "The Origins of Art," Fischer starts from the premise that human beings struggle to control nature and that it is in this process that the particularly human aspects of work develop. And work in turn, he argues, is the source and propelling element which develops communication and ultimately language:

By his work, man transforms the world like a magician . . . material objects are transformed into signs, names, and concepts; man himself is transformed from an animal into a man.

This magic is the very root of human existence, creating a sense of powerlessness and at the same time a consciousness of power, a fear of nature together with the ability to control nature, is the very essence of all art.

. . . .

Art was a magic tool, and it served man in mastering nature and developing social relationships. . . . The decisive function of art was to exert power—power over nature, an enemy, a sexual partner, power over reality, power to strengthen the human collective. Art in the dawn of humanity had little to do with "beauty" and nothing at all to do with any aesthetic desire: it was a magic tool or weapon of the human collective in its struggle for survival.[49]

Clearly, his intent is to synthesize an approach to art which will ground it inextricably in the most material of man's activities (work) and yet maintain within it a component that is mystical, abstract, and intuitive, preserving a special function for the artist.

The abstract historical sketch of human development which he presents suggests a pattern: as complex societies emerged, they destroyed innate tribal unity; however, Fischer argues that some of art's social and collective features remained from the tribal period. He suggests that a residual influence carries over even into societies with strong class structure, extensive divisions of labor, and individualism as the dominant ideology:

Even the most subjective artist works on behalf of society. By the sheer fact of describing feelings, relationships, and conditions that have not been described before, he channels them from the apparently isolated "I" into a "we," and this "we" can be recognized even in the brimming subjectivity of an artist's personality.

. . . .

Art itself is a social reality. Society needs the artist, that supreme sorcerer, and it has a right to demand of him that he should be conscious of his social function. . . .[50]

His conclusion is that art has not lost its social moorings but that "in class society the classes try to recruit art—that powerful voice of the collective—into serving their particular purposes." He argues that because of its traditional social orientation art has a special function: It "must show the world as changeable" and it must "help to change" the world. Not to do this is the ultimate surrender of the social function.

This social aspect of art and the social setting in which the artist creates is the second area of primary interest and leads to the issue of sociology and art—Marxist criticism of art is often labeled as sociological criticism. A penetrating analysis of the sociology of art is found in Arnold Hauser, *The Philosophy of Art History.*[51]

Hauser wants to illustrate the legitimacy of the sociological approach, especially in the face of those critics of the art for art's sake persuasion who believe that "any reference to actualities beyond the work must irretrievably destroy its aesthetic illusion." [52] More importantly, the point which he wishes to stress and which justifies the sociological approach is his belief that "all genuine art leads us by detour . . . back to reality in the end." Generally, Hauser's social views align with those of Fischer, but

Hauser suggests a special interpretation of the social connection while arguing for the validity of Marx's view that spiritual values are also political weapons. He believes that sociology serves this unique function:

Every honest attempt to discover the truth and depict things faithfully is a struggle against one's own subjectivity and partiality, one's individual and class interests; one can seek to become aware of these as a source of error, while realizing that they can never be finally excluded. . . . And the fact that there are such limits of objectivity is the ultimate and decisive justification for a sociology of culture; they stop up the last loophole by which we might hope to escape from the influence of social causation.[53]

Hauser recognizes that while all art is socially conditioned everything in art is not necessarily definable in sociological terms:

For sociology is subject to certain limitations common to all those disciplines, notably psychology, which employ the genetic method to deal with cultural forms, limitations arising out of that method. It is in fact likely to lose sight . . . of the work of art as such and to consider it a record of something more important than the work itself. . . . The sociological view of art is to be rejected only if it claims to be the sole legitimate point of view, and if it confuses the sociological importance of a work with aesthetic value.[54]

He is careful to note that limitations of sociological approaches do exist and suggests that the limitations become particularly obvious if the attempt is made to simplify, in a crude way, the essential complexity inherent in the art work. Essentially, he is refusing to accept the notion that there is a sociological equivalence to artistic excellence. He wants to preserve the "aesthetic experience" which makes art (for him) special, unique, and personal. Despite both the limitations and the warnings, he argues for the rationality of a sociological approach. Its rationality becomes the ultimate redeeming feature: "To recognize the claims of sociology is to decide in favor of a rational ordering of life and for a struggle against prejudices. The idea upon which this cardinal position of sociology is founded is the discovery of the ideological character of thought. . . ."[55]

Hauser is not sure that the sociological approach will uncover the kernel of aesthetic essence, but he suggests that if sociology is sensitively applied the success is more likely.

One such apparently sensitive approach is Lucien Goldmann's genetic-structuralist analysis, which represents an effort to connect ideology to art. Goldmann wants to establish what he calls a "scientific" method for the study of literary works. To this end, he tries to develop a dialectical method on a materialist base that shows an integration of the artist and his work into a social whole. Goldmann specifically attacks content-oriented "literary sociology." Its weaknesses, according to Goldmann, are: it tries to connect content to a previously defined "collective consciousness;" it cannot account for specific literary qualities; and it is often applied to secondary works which tend to be less creative and therefore less able to initiate an aesthetic response.[56]

The essence of Goldmann's structuralist approach is the *great* writer who creates in his imaginary universe a structure which corresponds most closely to the ideology or world outlook of a particular class. This is the basic difference between content-oriented and structuralist sociology. The former analyzes the work as a "reflection" of the collective consciousness of that group, while the latter sees the work as a "constituent element"—significantly contributing to the expression of a class outlook though not necessarily consciously.[57] Greatness is essential to Goldmann's argument because only certain social groups have "global visions," and these are the significant groups in determining the direction of society— either trying to preserve the status quo or to restructure it.

It is in the propaedeutic to his specific study of Pascal and Racine that the hypothesis is most clearly stated:

. . . any great literary or artistic work is the expression of a world vision. This vision is the product of a collective group consciousness which reaches its highest expression in the mind of a poet or a thinker. The expression which his work provides is then studied by the historian who uses the idea of the world vision as a tool which will help him to deduce two things from the text: the essential meaning of the work he is studying and the meaning which the individual and partial elements take on when the work is looked at as a whole.
. . . the method which consists of going from the actual text to the conceptual vision, and then returning from this vision to the text again, is not an innovation of dialectical materialism. The improvement which dialectical materialism makes upon this method lies in the fact that by integrating ideas of a particular individual into those of a social group, and especially by analyzing the historical function played in the genesis of ideas by social classes, it provides a scientific basis for the concept of world vision, and frees it from any criticism that it might be purely arbitrary, speculative and metaphysical.[58]

The doubleness of his dialectical method is based on what he calls "comprehension" and "explanation." Comprehension is illumination of specifics, and explanation is insertion of them into larger structures:

. . . to throw light on the tragic structure of Pascal's *Pensées* and Racinian theater is a process of *comprehending;* inserting them in extremist Jansenism, while setting forth the structure of the latter, is a process of comprehending the latter, but is a process of explaining the writings of Pascal and Racine; inserting extremist Jansenism into the global history of Jansenism is to explain the first and comprehend the latter. To insert Jansenism, as an ideologically expressive movement, into the history of the nobility of the robe of the seventeenth century is to explain Jansenism and comprehend the nobility of the robe. To insert the history of the nobility of the robe into the global history of French society is to explain it, while comprehending the latter, so on.[59]

However, Goldmann is an overly sophisticated thinker who has outlined a very abstract technique for understanding the ideological role of artists and of their individual works. He suggests that the ideas of an artist cannot be fully understood by studying the work in isolation. "Ideas," Goldmann comments, "are only a partial aspect of a less abstract reality: that of the whole, living man."[60] Real understanding of the ideas of an artist comes from an analysis of the social group to which he belongs—i.e., when the artist produces *great* art it can be shown that the work represents a whole social class. However, it is this presumption of greatness which is the most egregious inconsistency in Goldmann's hypothesis. It seems in fact to be another example of an arbitrary standard, because the aesthetic judgment of greatness occurs first within that larger social structure. Through this self-defining process he hopes to secure a clear statement of the global vision of the larger unit. It seems, therefore, that his "scientific" tool (capable of illuminating the artistic endeavor) is hopelessly enmeshed in and dominated by the larger structure.

A final example of the varieties of approaches to a Marxist interpretation is the application of dialectics to the study of literature. An interesting attempt is a work by Frederic Jameson, in which he postulates a theory for a dialectical (i.e., what he terms a Marxist) aesthetic based on analyses of European critics who use dialectics.[61]

There are two significant propositions in his work: (1) the assertion that dialectics is the most important contribution of Marxism—arguing for a rather direct connection of Marx to Hegel; and (2) the call for the academic acceptance of this variety of Marxist aesthetics.

Jameson believes that an Anglo-American tradition—what he calls the mixture of "political liberalism, empiricism, and logical positivism"—is bankrupt and that perhaps the only viable alternative is to accept the dialectical methods of the German and French critics:

For the bankruptcy of the liberal tradition is as plain on the philosophical level as it is on the political: which does not mean that it has lost its prestige or ideological potency. . . . It is therefore time for those of us in the sphere of influence of the Anglo-American tradition to learn to think dialectically, to acquire the rudiments of a dialectical culture and the essential critical weapons which it provides.[62]

Given this dead end, he believes it is important to understand the European critics in order to see and accept the wide variety of "Marxisms" which they present:

> For it is perfectly consistent with the spirit of Marxism—with the principle that thought reflects its concrete social situation—that there should exist several different Marxisms . . . one corresponds to the postrevolutionary industrial countries of the socialist bloc, another—a kind of peasant Marxism—to China and Cuba and the countries of the Third World, while yet another tries to deal theoretically with the unique questions raised by monopoly capitalism in the West. It is in the context of this last . . . Marxism that the great themes of Hegel's philosophy—the relationship of part to whole, the opposition between concrete and abstract, the concept of totality, the dialectic of appearance and essence, the interactions between subject and object—are once again the order of the day.[63]

The central purpose for the discussion of the various dialectical critics is to show the significance of their work and to provide several separate illustrations of an alternative to our stagnant philosophy. However, it is the extensive analytical essay at the conclusion of *Marxism and Form* that presents his theoretical construct. This essay is somewhat abstractly described as ". . . an evocation of dialectical literary criticism, and beyond it of dialectical thinking in general, as a form in time, as process, as a lived experience of a peculiar and determinate structure."[64]

The most direct approach to an understanding of Jameson's position is to outline the nature of explanation which he sees dialectics providing about literature and then to analyze the arguments which he uses to support such judgments. The basic literary question for Jameson is the relationship between content and form:

> In the long run, however, there is no need to justify the socio-economic "translation" which Marxism sees as the ultimate explanatory code for literary and cultural phenomena. Such justification is already implicit in the dialectical notion of the relationship between form and content. . . . For the essential characteristic of literary raw material or latent content is precisely that it never really is initially formless, never . . . initially contingent, but is rather already meaningful from the outset, being neither more nor less than the very components of our concrete social life itself: words, thoughts, objects, desires, people, places, activities. The work of art does not confer meanings on these elements, but rather transforms their initial meanings into some new and heightened construction of meaning. . . .
> What we have called interpretation is therefore a misnomer: content does not need to be treated or interpreted, precisely because it is essentially and immediately meaningful in itself. . . . . Content is already concrete, in that it is essentially social and historical experience. . . . Thus the process of criticism is not so much an interpretation of content as a revealing of it. . . .[65]

The task or burden of dialectical criticism is to unify the understanding of form and content in an effort to explain social reality and individual experience:

> The works of culture come to us as signs in an all-but-forgotten code, as symptoms of diseases no longer even recognized as such, as fragments of a totality we have long since lost the organs to see. . . . The literary fact, like other objects that make up our social reality, cries out for commentary, for interpretation, for decipherment, for diagnosis.[66]

His argument is advanced with the assumption that in the historical situation of a dominant middle class society based on commodity production, only a method of investigation which uncovers the mystifying elements and explains the historical circumstances and connections can unravel contradictions. This system is, of course, what Jameson calls dialectics.

> The dialectic is designed to eject us from this illusory order, to project us in spite of ourselves out of our concepts into the world of genuine realities to which those concepts were supposed to apply. We cannot, of course, ever really get outside our own subjectivities: to think so is the illusion of positivism.
> . . . In the context of our present description, which limited itself to an account of the dialectic as a mental operation, dialectical thinking proves to be a moment in which thought rectifies itself, in which the mind, suddenly drawing back and including itself in its new and widened apprehension, doubly restores and *regrounds* its earlier notions in a new glimpse of reality: first, through a coming to consciousness of the way in which our conceptual instruments themselves determine the shape and limits of the results arrived at (the Hegelian dialectic); and thereafter, in that second and more concrete movement of reflection which is the specifically Marxist form, in a consciousness of ourselves as at once the product and the producer of history, and of the profoundly historical character of our socio-economic situation as it informs both solutions and the problems which give rise to them equally.[67]

The primacy of Hegel over Marx, in terms of establishing an understanding both of aesthetics and of history, is the fundamental assumption underlying this interpretation. According to Jameson, literature must be viewed in a double way: as a unique and autonomous structure and as part of a series of sequential developments. He interprets the Hegelian mode of analysis as isolating a literary category—the autonomous object of study (image, style, point of view, character, etc.)—to ". . .a succession of alternative structural realizations which we have called the diachronic sequence or construct, and which, always implied in the very intuition of the category itself, constitutes the concrete working out of the latter by the critic."[68]

He sees the limitation to the Hegelian approach: that by giving these categories a diachronic or historical sequence one does not remove them from the realm of ideal constructs. It is the shift to the concrete that is the contribution Marx adds and that characterizes what Jameson calls the Marxian mode of analysis. He suggests that Marx's contribution is more easily seen when the Hegelian diachronic sequence is expressed as a contradiction between form and content.

. . . what is most striking about the distinction between form and content is that despite the enormous range of phenomena to which it will be applied, the concept is essentially aesthetic in origin . . . from materials which belong essentially to the superstructure. This is, indeed, the secret of its enormous force in Marx's hands: for what is relatively transparent and demonstrable in the cultural realm, namely that change is essentially a function of content seeking its expression in form, is precisely what is unclear in the reified world of political, social, and economic realities.[69]

However, in arguing the primacy of Hegel, Jameson concludes that Hegel in his *Aesthetik* merges intrinsic and extrinsic criticism into a unified (though dialectical) analysis and that this merger is the beginning of a criticism rooted in social and historical reality. Further, he suggests that Hegel, in measuring the correspondence of content to form, provides a precise index to the historical moment:

The logic of content is *in the long run* . . . social and historical in character . . . . To articulate the relationship between artistic fact as such and the larger social and historical reality to which it corresponds requires a gradual enlargement of critical focus. . . . To omit this enlargement, this movement from the intrinsic to the extrinsic, is itself an ideological act, to the degree to which it encourages belief in some ahistorical essence of art and of cultural activity in general.[70]

Stated, then, in an oversimplified way, Jameson's view posits two separate modes of analysis, Hegelian and Marxian, connected in a very special linkage.

This particular relationship between Hegel and Marx rests on an interpretation that presents Marx as a corrective to Hegel; it opposes the notion that Marx overturned Hegel.[71] Jameson suggests that Marx, in uncovering the infrastructure of society through an economic interpretation, is "simply the sign of the approach to the concrete. The middle class world is therefore the common object of all historical meditation." [72] And since Marx clearly states in *The German Ideology,* according to Jameson, that elements of the superstructure have no history of their own, he concludes that the best way to approach literature is through a dialectical criticism which combines Hegel's diachronic sequence with Marx's revelation of the concrete. He suggests that dialectical criticism forces the critic to include history and that in some mystical way dialectical criticism grounded in Hegel and Marx is ipso facto historical: ". . . dialectical thinking is doubly historical: not only are the phenomena with which it works historical in character, but it must unfreeze the very concepts with which they have been understood, and interpret the very immobility of the latter as unhistorical phenomena in their own right." [73] Jameson also argues that in the process of selecting out (isolating) the literary category to be analyzed in the context of the individual work of art and the "diachronic sequence" of its development, one will uncover "concrete reality." [74]

The central weaknesses are several. First, Jameson never explains how one achieves "concrete history." While arguing for historical precision, his analysis is almost totally ahistorical. His belief that the dialectical method forces one to include history is not illustrated by example. (It seems that dialectics becomes a mind game and at one point he even refers to dialectics as "thought to the second power.") This attempt to spin an aesthetic from intellectual fibers stretching from Hegel through Marx is presented in total isolation from any specific historical example. There is no example and not even an outline suggesting how such an example would be isolated and studied.

Somewhat more disturbing than his approach to history is his attitude toward literature and literary criticism. On the latter, he argues that dialectical criticism differentiates itself from all absolutist theories of aesthetics:

For a genuinely dialectical criticism, indeed, there can be no pre-established categories of analysis: to the degree that each work is the end result of a kind of inner logic or development of its own content, it evolves its own categories and dictates the specific terms of its own interpretation. Thus dialectical criticism is at the other extreme from all single-shot or univalent aesthetic theories which seek the same structure in all works of art and prescribe for them a single type of interpretive technique or a single mode of explanation. [75]

On literature he is also at times self-contradictory. While rejecting any Marxism that would try to claim a scientific approach to history or society, he notes that literature provides a closed system (a situation very much like a laboratory, I guess); literature ". . . offers a privileged microcosm in which to observe dialectical thinking at work." [76] Why is it a particularly good microcosm? He never explains. He treats other critics who analyze literature directly, but his own theoretical essay never examines closely or comprehensively any literature. He sidesteps such analyses even while acknowledging that it is only through actual literary analysis in practice that one can show dialectical thinking at work. His own assumption about literature as a laboratory is arbitrary; he has not broken from the absolutist position which he attacks. He has presented no basis for a literary criticism.

The overview of these three basic tendencies suggests, I believe, that critics and philosophers cannot, with armchair theorizing alone, develop a Marxist aesthetics. In my view, the key to understanding a Marxist approach to art and culture rests not on theory but on practice, and as I suggest in the body of this book a more useful approach may be found in a narrow historical study of a specific party in a circumscribed period.

NOTES

INTRODUCTION

1. On the 1930s, see especially Walter B. Rideout, *The Radical Novel in the United States, 1900-1954: Some Interrelations of Literature and Society* (New York, 1956); Daniel Aaron, *Writers on the Left* (New York, 1965); Irving Howe and Lewis Coser, *The American Communist Party: A Critical History, 1919-1957* (Boston, 1957); Joseph Starobin, *American Communism in Crisis, 1943-57* (Cambridge, Mass., 1972); and James B. Gilbert, *Writers and Partisans: A History of Literary Radicalism in America* (New York, 1968).

2. Norman Markowitz, "A View from the Left: From the Popular Front to Cold War Liberalism," in Robert Griffith and Athan Theoharis, eds., *The Specter: Original Essays on the Cold War and the Origins of McCarthyism* (New York, 1974), pp. 99-100.

3. Philip Rahv, "Proletarian Literature: A Political Autopsy," *Southern Review* 4 (winter 1939); 618.

1: THE STALIN MYTH AND SOVIET CULTURE

1. For a discussion of literary terminology (realism, naturalism, socialist realism), see George J. Becker, ed., *Documents of Modern Literary Realism* (Princeton, N.J., 1963).

2. Merle Fainsod, *How Russia Is Ruled* (Cambridge, Mass., 1963, rev. ed.), pp. 577-79.

3. Robert Slusser, *American Historical Review* 79 (June 1974): 820-22.

4. David Joravsky's introductory essay to Roy A. Medvedev, *Let History Judge: The Origins and Consequences of Stalinism* (New York, 1971), p. xi.

5. Christopher Hill, "The Monster and His Myths," *New York Review of Books* 20 (January 24, 1974): 9 ff.

6. Robert H. McNeal, "Trotsky's Interpretation of Stalin," *Canadian Slavonic Papers* 5 (1961): 87.

7. Hill, p. 9.

8. Roger Pethybridge's review of Ronald Hingley, *Joseph Stalin: Man and Legend* (New York, 1974), in *Slavic Review* 35 (March 1976): 136.

9. For a positive and controversial view of Stalin, see Bruce Franklin, ed., *The*

124 / NOTES

Essential Stalin: Major Theoretical Writings, 1905-1952 (New York, 1972), the introduction, pp. 1-38.
10.   Sheila Fitzpatrick, "Culture and Politics under Stalin: A Reappraisal," *Slavic Review* 35 (June 1976): 211-31.
11.   Ibid., p. 230.
12.   Gleb Struve, *Russian Literature under Lenin and Stalin, 1917-1953* (Norman, Okla., 1970), p. 276.
13.   Ibid., p. 91.
14.   Ibid., p. 221.
15.   Ibid., pp. 253-54.
16.   Ibid., p. 255.
17.   Ibid.
18.   A significant exception is, of course, Max Eastman's famous essay attacking Stalin for regimenting both art and artists. See his *Artists in Uniform* (New York, 1934).
19.   George Reavey and Marc Slonim, eds., *Soviet Literature: An Anthology* (London, 1933), p. 45.
20.   George Reavey, *Soviet Literature Today* (New York, 1947, 1969), p. 18.
21.   Ibid., p. 19.
22.   Marc Slonim, *Soviet Russian Literature: Writers and Problems* (New York, 1964), pp. 159-61.
23.   Max Hayward, introduction to Max Hayward and Leopold Labedz, eds., *Literature and Revolution in Soviet Russia, 1917-1962: A Symposium* (London, 1963), p. vii. Other standard overviews from this perspective are Alexander Kaun, *Soviet Poets and Poetry* (Los Angeles, 1943); E. J. Simmons, *An Outline of Modern Russian Literature, 1880-1940* (Ithaca, N.Y., 1943). Of course, an important source for these writers was Leon Trotsky's *Literature and Revolution* (Ann Arbor, Mich., 1971, 1924.)
24.   Harold Swayze, *Political Control of Literature in the U.S.S.R., 1946-1959* (Cambridge, Mass., 1962), p. 123.
25.   Ibid., pp. 24-25. For similar approaches, see R. M. Hankin, "Soviet Literary Controls," in E. J. Simmons, ed., *Continuity and Change in Russian and Soviet Thought* (Cambridge, Mass., 1955); and E. J. Simmons's introduction, "Soviet Literature and Controls" in his *Through the Glass of Soviet Literature: Views of Russian Society* (New York, 1953).

2: FROM PROLETARIANISM TO SOCIALIST REALISM

1.   See Sheila Fitzpatrick, *The Commissariat of Enlightenment: Soviet Organization of Education and the Arts under Lunacharsky, October 1917-1921* (Cambridge, England, 1970).
2.   See R. A. Maguire, *Red Virgin Soil: Soviet Literature in the 1920s* (Princeton, N.J., 1968).
3.   See R. A. Maguire, "Literary Conflicts in the 1920s," *Survey* (winter 1972), pp. 98-127.
4.   For insight into the theoretical debates, one must note the general decline in popularity of Plekhanov's theories. See Swayze, ch. 1, "The Theoretical Foundations of Literary Controls," pp. 1-25; and see Burton Rubin, "Plekhanov and Soviet Literary Criticism," *American Slavic and East European Review* 15 (1956); 527-42.
5.   For a complete development of this hypothesis, see Edward J. Brown, *The Proletarian Episode in Russian Literature, 1928-1932* (New York, 1953).
6.   See Herman Ermolaev, *Soviet Literary Theories, 1917-1934: The Genesis of Socialist Realism* (Berkeley, Calif., 1963). For a complete exegesis of both Brown and Ermolaev, see Lawrence H. Schwartz, "The CPUSA's Approach to Literature in the 1930s: Socialist Realism and the American Party's 'line' on Literature," (dissertation, Rutgers University, 1977), pp. 39-75.

7.   See Sheila Fitzpatrick, ed., *Cultural Revolution in Russia, 1928-1931* (Bloomington, Ind., 1978).
8.   Ibid., p. 4.
9.   Sheila Fitzpatrick, "Cultural Revolution as Class War," in *Cultural Revolution in Russia, 1928-1931,* p. 29.
10.   Ibid., p. 36.
11.   Ibid., pp. 37-38.
12.   Ibid., p. 38.
13.   Ibid., p. 11.
14.   Sheila Fitzpatrick, "Culture and Politics under Stalin: A Reappraisal," *Slavic Review* 35 (June 1976); p. 218.
15.   See Sheila Fitzpatrick's three articles covering the 1922-32 period: "The 'Soft' Line on Culture and Its Enemies: Soviet Cultural Policy, 1922-27," *Slavic Review* 33 (June 1974): 267-87; "The Emergence of Glaviskusstvo: Class War on the Cultural Front, Moscow, 1928-29," *Soviet Studies* 23 (October 1971): 236-53; and "Cultural Revolution in Russia 1928-32," *Journal of Contemporary History* 9 (January 1974): 32-52.
16.   Resolution of the Central Committee, April 23, 1932. Reprinted in Brown, pp. 200-1.
17.   Reprinted in Brown, pp. 201-2.
18.   Joseph Stalin, *Selected Writings* (New York, 1940), pp. 215-16.
19.   Brown, pp. 215-16; Ermolaev, pp. 133 ff.
20.   See *Sovetskaya literatura na novam etape: stenogramma pervova plenuma orgkomiteta soyuza sovetskikh pisatelei, October 29-November 3, 1932* (Moscow, 1933), especially the speeches of Gronsky, Kirpotin, and Subotsky. See also Brown, pp. 209 and 218, and Harold Swayze, *Political Control of Literature in the U.S.S.R., 1946-1959* (Cambridge Mass., 1962), p. 116.
21.   Ermolaev, p. 197.
22.   *Pervy vsesoyuzny syezd sovetskikh pisatelei, Stenograficheski otchyhat* (Moscow, 1934), p. 716. The rules of the union appear as appendix 8, pp. 716-18, in this volume.
23.   Ibid., p. 716. Interestingly, in order to qualify for membership the rules carefully state that one must be a professional, working writer.
24.   Bruce Franklin, ed., *The Essential Stalin: Major Theoretical Writings, 1905-1952* (New York, 1972), pp. 274-96. For specific changes in rules and membership requirements, see Robert H. McNeal, ed., *Resolutions and Decisions of the CPSU* vol. 3: *The Stalin Years, 1929-53* (Toronto, 1974), pp. 131-53.
25.   L. M. Kaganovich, *Report on the Organizational Problem of Party and Soviet Construction* (Moscow, 1934), p. 152.
26.   Ibid., pp. 151-52.
27.   For a collection of the major speeches, see H. G. Scott, ed., *Problems of Soviet Literature: Reports and Speeches at the First Soviet Writers' Congress* (London, 1935).
28.   Ibid., pp. 263 and 265.

3: THE VIEW FROM AMERICA

1.   Moissaye J. Olgin, "A Pageant of Soviet Literature: The All-Union Writers' Congress in Moscow,"*NM* 13, no. 3 (October 16, 1934): 16-20, and "One Literature of Many Tongues: The All-Union Writers' Congress," *NM* 13, no. 4 (October 23, 1934): 16-19.
2.   "First All-Union Congress of Soviet Writers," in Henry Hart, ed., *American Writers' Congress,* (New York, 1935), pp. 45-51. Olgin incorrectly attributes to Stalin the coining of the term "socialist realism." He also inaccurately claims that RAPP was dissolved by Stalin's initiative and because there was no longer a need for a special proletarian organization.

3. Robert Gessner, "A Task for the Writers' Congress," *NM* 15, no. 1 (April 2, 1935): 39-41.

4. Edwin Seaver, "Socialist Realism" in the Review and Comment section, *NM* 17, no. 4 (October 22, 1935): 23-24. Mr. Seaver in a conversation with the author (June 1976) seemed somewhat surprised when reminded of this piece, since he claimed little special knowledge of socialist realism either as a literary technique or as a political reorganization.

5. On the distance between America and the Soviet Union on literary issues, see the symposium "Where We Stand," *International Literature* no. 3 (July 1934): 80-94.

6. The Kharkov resolution is reprinted in *The Literature of the World Revolution*, special number (1931), p. 86. (This entire issue of the journal is devoted to the proceedings of the conference.)

7. Ibid., p. 88.

8. Ibid., pp. 90-93. And on fellow travelers, see pp. 88-91. The IURW does formulate a rather detailed critique of the *New Masses* for the year 1931. The thirteen-point review is comprehensive and detailed. It is the first and last such direct analysis. It attempts to assess how well the magazine fulfilled the goals set at Kharkov to change it from an organ of radicalism to one of proletarian culture. See IURW, "Resolution on the Work of the New Masses for 1931," *NM* 8, no. 3 (September 1932): 20-21. Also see an expanded version of this critique by A. Elistratova, "New Masses," *International Literature* no. 1 (1932): 107-14.

9. For the American resolutions at the Kharkov Conference, see *The Literature of the World Revolution*, special number (1931), pp. 121-22. In *NM* see 6, no. 9 (February 1931): 2 and 5-8; and see Michael Gold, "Notes from Kharkov," *NM* 6 no. 10 (March 1931): 4-6.

10. See *NM* 7 (May 1931): 22. See also *DW*, May 9, 1931, p. 6; February 18, 1932, p. 1; April 14, 1932, p. 2; and April 23, 1932, p. 4.

11. See *NM* 7 no. 2 (June 1931): 22. See also *DW*, June 2, 1931, p. 4, and June 13, 1931, p. 4. On the literary service, see a review by Conrad Komorowski in *NM* 8, no. 3 (September 1932): 27-28, and a review and criticism of the service by A. B. Magil in *DW*, September 14, 1932, p. 4.

12. See "Draft Manifesto of the John Reed Club," *NM* 7, no. 12 (June 1932): 3-4. On the adoption of the Kharkov program by the JRC, see Oakley Johnson, "The John Reed Club Convention," *NM* 8, no. 1 (July 1932): 14-15; and also see *DW*, May 4, 1932, p. 2, and June 2, 1932, p. 3. On the growth of the JRC, see Mike Gold's column "What a World," *DW*, October 10, 1933, p. 5.

13. See Joseph Freeman, "Ivory Towers—White and Red, Part 2: Perspectives of 1932," *NM* 12, no. 11 (September 11, 1934): 21-23. See also *DW*, October 7, 1933, p. 7, and December 21, 1933, p. 5. For the announcement of goals for the new weekly and the growth of new proletarian magazines, see the editorial statement *NM* 10, no. 1 (January 2, 1934): 3 and 7. For analysis of the first issue of *NM* as a weekly, see Sender Garlin, "Inheritor of Most Vital Revolutionary Tradition in America," *DW*, January 6, 1934, p. 7. On the growth of proletarian magazines, see the announcement of the forthcoming *Partisan Review* in *DW*, January 23, 1934, p. 5. And for a review of its first issue, see Isidor Schneider, *DW*, February 8, 1934, p. 5.

14. On the creation of the Professional Groups for Foster and Ford, see *DW*, October 13, 1932, p. 3. The manifesto of this group was published as a pamphlet, "Culture and the Crisis: An Open Letter to the Writers, Artists, Teachers, Physicians, Engineers, Scientists, and Professional Workers of America" (New York, 1932).

15. Max Eastman, "Artists in Uniform," *Modern Monthly* 7, no. 7 (August 1933): 397-404, and his book *Artists in Uniform: A Study in Literature and Bureaucratism* (1934).

16. For an early party debate over the problems associated with the issues involved in the Kharkov resolutions—the proper role for fellow travelers, the definition of

proletarian literature, the function of Marxist criticism, etc.—see Philip Rahv, "The Literary Class War," *NM* 8, no. 2 (August 1932): 7-10 and A. B. Magil's response, "Pity and Terror," *NM* 8, no. 5 (December 1932): 16-19.

17. Joshua Kunitz, "Choose Your Uniform," *NM* 8, no. 12 (August 1933): 14.

18. Joshua Kunitz, "Max Eastman's Hot Unnecessary Tears," *NM* 9, no. 1 (September 1933): 14.

19. Ibid., p. 15.

20. Joshua Kunitz, "A Note on Max Eastman," *NM* 11, no. 6 (May 8, 1934): 25. The disinterest in organizational changes is also reflected in a series of articles Kunitz writes during the summer of 1934 discussing Russian literature of the 1920s. The six-part series entitled "Literary Wars in the USSR" ran in the *NM* from June to August 1934.

21. Leon Dennen, "Bunk by a Bohemian," *PR* 1, no. 3 (June-July 1934): 22-26. Dennen was especially upset by Eastman's idea that Stalin controlled literature. His comments are of special interest because he did attend the opening session of the Organizing Committe for the Soviet Writer's Union which met in October-November 1932.

22. The implication is that the Party destroyed the JRC and with it proletarian literature in favor of a larger, more "united front" organization. In essence, the argument is that the Party no longer found the JRC a convenient tool and shifted to another in which more famous and published writers could be cultivated at the expense of the younger and more proletarian writers. On this view of the dissolution of the JRC, see two retrospective articles by former thirties radicals: William Phillips, "What Happened in the '30s," *Commentary* 34, no. 3 (September 1962): 201-12 (especially p. 205), and Daniel Aaron's symposium "Thirty Years Later: Memories of the First American Writers' Congress," *American Scholar* 35 (1965): 495-551 (the participants were Malcolm Cowley, Kenneth Burke, Granville Hicks, and William Phillips).

23. For reports on the National John Reed Club conference and Trachtenberg's proposal, see "National John Reed Club Conference," *PR* 1, no. 5 (November-December 1934): 60-61; Orrick Johns, "The John Reed Clubs Meet," *NM* 13, no. 5 (October 30, 1934): 25-26; Alan Calmer, "A New Period in American Leftwing Literature," *International Literature* no. 7 (1935): 73-75. For *PR's* editorial endorsement of the congress, see *PR* 2, no. 6 (February-March 1935): 94-96. As a matter of fact, the dissident *Partisan Review* crowd does not attack the idea of a writers' congress and the formation of the League of American Writers until 1938. See Philip Rahv, "Two Years of Progress: From Waldo Frank to Donald Ogden Stewart," *PR* 4, no. 3 (February 1938): 22-30, and also his "Proletarian Literature: A Political Autopsy," *Southern Review* 4, (winter 1939): 616-28. The earliest reference to the weakening of proletarian culture by the shift to the LAW is in Alan Calmer, "Portrait of the Artist as Proletarian," *Saturday Review of Literature* 16 (July 31, 1937): 3 ff. The most famous story claiming that the JRC were dissolved by fiat is by Richard Wright in Crossman's *The God That Failed* (New York, 1965), pp. 122-23.

24. "Call for an American Writers' Congress," *NM* 14, no. 4 (January 22, 1935): 20. Compare with the draft manifesto prepared by the New York City JRC for the 1932 JRC Organizing Conference, "Draft Manifesto of John Reed Clubs," *NM* 7, no. 12 (June 1932): 3-4.

25. There is a great temptation to argue that this first Writers' Congress in some way is a precursor to the new line. But there is no evidence to support it.

26. For the view that intellectuals were moving left and that there was a marked decrease in sectarian attitudes of Communists, see Freeman, pp. 20-24, published before the JRC Conference. Granville Hicks also saw a very specific function for the small JRC magazines: "Our Magazines and Their Functions," *NM* 13, no. 12 (December 18, 1934), 22-23. For his view of the expansion of proletarian fiction in 1934, see "Revolutionary Literature of 1934," *NM* 14, no. 1 (January 1, 1935): 36-38. And finally see the collection Granville Hicks, et. al., eds., *Proletarian*

Literature in the United States: An Anthology (New York, 1935).

4: AMERICAN INTELLECTUALS AND THE PARTY

1. See the table of contents and "Who's Who," *NM* 21, no. 12 (December 15, 1935): 2.
2. Ralph Bates, quoted in Frank A. Warren's *Liberals and Communism: The Red Decade Revisited* (Bloomington, Ind., 1966); for his view of the impact of the Moscow trials and the collapse of the popular front after the pact, see pp. 163-215.
3. Malcolm Cowley reported the resignation of 100 of the 800 members of the LAW and one-third of the group's elected officers after the pact announcement: *New Republic* 104 (August 26, 1940): 279-80.
4. All the standard secondary sources treat the trials and the pact conspicuously and especially enjoy check-listing the refugees from Communism. For example, see Daniel Bell, *Marxian Socialism in the United States* (Princeton, N.J., 1967), pp. 150-52.
5. See Richard Pells, *Radical Visions and American Dreams* (New York, 1973), pp. 151-80, 187-93, and 292-329.
6. In addition to standard secondary sources, see Norman H. Pearson, "The Nazi-Soviet Pact and the End of a Dream," in Richard Abrams and Lawrence Levine, *The Shaping of Twentieth-Century America: Interpretative Essays,* 2nd ed. (Boston, 1971), pp. 438-54; and see also David Caute, *The Fellow Travellers: A Postscript to the Enlightenment* (New York, 1973). Exemplary of the memoirs of redemption is Granville Hicks, *Where We Came Out* (New York, 1954) and *Part of the Truth* (New York, 1964).
7. V. J. Jerome, "Unmasking an American Revisionist," *C* 12, no. 1 (January 1933): 82. See also Earl Browder, "The Revisionism of Sidney Hook," *C* 12, no. 2 (February 1933): 133-46, and the conclusion in the March number, pp. 285-300. Within one year Hook had helped to organize Muste's American Workers Party.
8. For Browder's speech see Henry Hart, ed., *American Writers' Congress* (New York, 1935), "Communism and Literature," pp. 66-70. For a collection of Browder's thoughts on culture, see *Pamphlets by Earl Browder,* vol. 1 (n.d.): pamphlet no. 6, "Communism and Culture," a collection of speeches and writings from 1935 to 1941 (New York, 1941).
9. Hart, p. 70.
10. The best overview of the controversy with intellectuals about the trials and Spain is found in the *New Masses 1936-1939.* Comprehensive coverage of the Spanish War begins with a special issue of *NM,* 22, no. 5 (January 26, 1937).
11. For the transcript of the major speeches see Henry Hart, ed., *The Writer in a Changing World* (New York, 1937). The call to the second congress is reprinted in *NM* 23, no. 7 (May 4, 1937): 25.
12. This speech is reprinted in Earl Browder, *The People's Front* (New York, 1938), pp. 276-81. See p. 276.
13. Ibid., p. 281.
14. William Z. Foster, "The Communist Party and the Professionals," *C* 17, no. 9 (September 1938): 805-10.
15. Ibid., p. 805.
16. Ibid., pp. 808-9.
17. Ibid., p. 806. For an analysis of the mistakes of the Socialist Party in dealing with middle class professionals and what is different now that the CP is in the lead, see pp. 806-7.
18. For discussions of drama and Communism in the 1930s see Jane D. Mathews, *The Federal Theatre, 1935-39: Plays, Relief and Politics* (Princeton, N.J. 1967); Gerald Rabkin, *Drama and Commitment: Politics in the American Theatre of the Thirties* (Bloomington, Ind., 1964); and Morgan Y. Himmelstein, *Drama Was a Weapon: The Left-Wing Theatre in N.Y., 1929-1941* (New Brunswick, N.J., 1963).

For analyses of the writers' projects, see Jerre Mangione, *The Dream and the Deal: The Federal Writers' Project, 1935-1943* (New York, 1972); Kathleen O'Connor McKinzie, "Writers on Relief, 1935-1942" (Ph.D. dissertation, Indiana University, 1970); and Monty N. Penkower, "The Federal Writers' Project: A Study in the Government Patronage of the Arts" (Ph.D. dissertation, Columbia University, 1970).

19. See Mike Gold, *The Hollow Men* (New York, 1941), especially chs. 3 and 4: "Renegades: A Warning of the End," and "War: The Final Curtain." See also Samuel Sillen, "Authors of Surrender," *NM* 37, no. 3 (October 8, 1940): 4-7; and "The Choice Before Us," *NM* 37, no. 11 (December 3, 1940), 17-18. For the best-known response, see V. J. Jerome, *Intellectuals and the War* (New York, 1940), especially chs. 2, 3, and 4. And for an early historical overview of the intellectual's role in defending democracy, see excerpts from Joseph Freeman's speech to the Third Writers' Congress in Donald O. Stewart, *Fighting Words*, (New York, 1940) pp. 149-58.

20. See Mike Gold's speech to the Fourth Congress of American Writers in Mike Folsom, ed., *Mike Gold: A Literary Anthology* (New York, 1972), entitled "The Second American Renaissance," p. 249.

21. Ibid., pp. 249 and 253.

22. Ibid., pp. 247-53.

23. Jerome, *Intellectuals*, pp. 58-63.

24. Gold, *The Hollow Men*, p. 128, and Jerome, *Intellectuals*, p. 15.

5: INTELLECTUALS AND THE PARTY LINE

1. The rather substantial discussion on this question in *DW* during the winter and spring of 1935 is rarely cited. For a general discussion of the many issues involved with this congress, see Mike Gold's column "Change the World" (he is especially interested in the problem of joining together writers and workers), January 23, p. 5; February 2, p. 7; February 4, p. 7; April 15, p. 5; April 24, p. 5; April 26, p. 5; May 1, p. 5; and May 9, p. 5. On middle class intellectuals and fascism, see Joseph North, "Disillusioned Intellectuals Must Be Won Over," *DW*, February 13, p. 5; and a reply by Jack Martin, "The Intellectuals As Friend and Ally," April 8, p. 5; Earl Conant, "Starvation and Misery Forcing Writers to Flee Ivory Towers," March 20, p. 5; and Joseph North, "The New Masses: A Weapon against War and Fascism," April 20, p. 7. On workers and writers, see Paul Peters, "On Writing and Selecting Plays for Workers," *DW*, February 27, p. 5; Walter Snow's letter in Gold's column, February 27, p. 5; "New Book Union Formed to Spread Vital Revolutionary Literature," April 9, p. 5; Myra Page, "Workers and Our Books," April 13, p. 7; Ben Field, "American Workers Can Create Literature," April 24, p. 5; and Alexander Trachtenberg, "Forge the Alliance of Workers and Writers," April 25, p. 5. On the congress itself, see "Mass Leaders and Prominent Authors Hail First AWC," *DW*, April 25, p. 5; "5,000 Great Writers Who Pledge Fight on Fascism and War," April 29, p. 3 (Browder's address is also printed on this page); "Authors' Congress Forms League of American Writers," *DW*, April 30, p. 2.

2. Editoral, *DW*, April 26, 1935, p. 6.

3. Edwin Seaver, "Writers Lead Defense of American Culture, . . . " *DW*, June 9, 1937, p. 7.

4. Ibid.

5. On *NM* and the middle class, see the special quarterly issue pushing for trade union organizing for professionals as the crisis "shatters illusions": *NM* 19, no. 2 (April 7, 1936). On *NM* and the proletarian magazines, see Alexander Trachtenberg "Partisan Review and Proletarian Literature," *DW*, March 11, 1936, p. 7.

6. On western writers, see reports of their meetings: Isidor Schneider, "Western Writers Make History," *NM* 21, no. 8 (November 17, 1936): 16; western writers' five-point program, *NM* 21, no. 11 (December 8, 1936): 2. For a report of the March 1, 1937, Western Writers' Congress (in preparation for the second AWC),

see *DW,* March 2, 1937, p. 7. The best overview of the 1935-36 period is *NM's* twenty-fifth anniversary issue, 21, no. 12 (December 15, 1936).

7. "Stewart Elected Head of Writers' Congress," *DW,* June 8, 1937, p. 3.

8. "Writers' Congress: League of American Writers Issues Call to Its Third Congress," *NM* 31, no. 8 (May 16, 1939): 17. For the program of the congress and a more general discussion of its themes and sessions, see *Direction* 2, no. 3 (May-June 1939).

9. Samuel Sillen, "American Writers, 1935 to 1939," *NM* 31, no. 13 (June 20, 1939): 22.

10. Ibid.

11. *TC* 17, no. 6 (June 1938): 562-70. And on the Pepper-Coffee bill and the general attempt to sustain the Federal Arts program, see Hallie Flanagan, *Arena: The History of the Federal Theatre* (New York, 1940), pp. 333-73.

12. Sillen, p. 24. See also Samuel Sillen, "The People, Yes," *NM* 31, no. 11 (June 6, 1939): 22-23, and Vincent Sheean's address to the Congress, "Ivory Tower for Rent," *NM* 31, no. 12 (June 13, 1939): 8.

13. "The Official Program of the Third American Writers' Congress," *Direction* 2, no. 3 (May-June 1939): 22-23.

14. Quoted in Donald O. Stewart, *Fighting Words,* ch. 7, "Hollywood Brigade," p. 116.

15. Ibid., pp. 107-09.

16. Joseph North, "The New Hollywood," *NM* 32, no. 2 (July 4, 1939): pp. 3-6.

17. Idem., *NM* 32, no. 3 (July 11, 1939): 15.

18. Ibid., pp. 14-16. For the detail of the corruption in the craft workers' International Alliance of Theatrical and Stage Employees (IATSE), see Ella Winter, "Show Business Showdown," *NM* 32, no. 9 (August 22, 1939): 7-8, and "Bill Bioff and the IATSE," *NM* 32, no. 10 (August 29, 1939): 10-11. For one screenwriter's positive view of the work of the league in Hollywood, see Arnaud d'Usseau, "Screen Writer Speaks," *NM* 32, no. 12 (September 12, 1939): 29-31. On SWG, see Ella Winter, "Screen Writers Close Ranks," *NM* 33, no. 2 (October 3, 1939): 27-29.

19. For a view of the 1930s cinema as basically escapist and conservative, see Richard Pells, *Radical Visions and American Dreams* (New York, 1973), pp. 263-91.

20. The problem of radio was considered in a special session. See Stewart, ch. 6, "Aerial Assault." Also treated separately was the Negro writer. And in a highly critical speech Langston Hughes deplored the paucity of Negroes who make their living as professionals. He suggested that there was little or no opportunity for Negroes to write for major publications or publishers and that Hollywood was even worse, See Stewart, pp. 58-63.

21. John Howard Lawson, "Writers' Trade Union," *Direction* 2 (May-June 1939): 18. On the issue of the relationship between the Authors' League and the LAW and on the background of the Authors' League, see George Albee, "The Writers' Organizations," *Directions* 1 (December 1938): 6 ff.

22. Stewart, ch. 8, "Marching Formation," pp. 122-24. On screen and radio writers, see pp. 134-39.

23. Stewart, p. 167.

24. Samuel Sillen, "Three Decades," *NM* 38, no. 9 (February 18, 1941): 8-10.

25. Earl Browder, "The Great Tradition," *NM* 38, no. 10 (February 25, 1941): 5-6.

6: POLITICS IN THE 1930s

1. Georgi Dimitrov, *United Front Against Fascism: Speeches Delivered at the Seventh World Congress of the Communist International* (New York, 1935), p. 29.

2. Ibid., p. 34. Emphasis in original.

3. Ibid., p. 93.

4. Ibid., p. 40.

5. Browder coined the phrase in an article "Americanism: Who Are the Americans?" *NM* 15, no. 13 (June 25, 1935): 15. This was part of a series of essays on "What Is Communism?" which was expanded into a book *What Is Communism?* (New York, 1935).

6. Earl Browder, "Concerning American Revolutionary Traditions," *The Communist* 17, no. 12 (December 1938): 1082.

7. Ibid., p. 1084.

8. William Z. Foster, *Toward Soviet America* (New York, 1932), p. 252. It is also important to see this book as part of the Party propaganda effort during the 1932 Foster/Ford election campaign.

9. "An Open Letter, as adopted by the Extraordinary National Conference of the Communist Party of the U.S.A., New York City, July 7-10, 1933," was first printed in *DW,* July 13, 1933, pp. 1 ff.

10. The development of the policy on work in large factories, of the social fascist strategy, and of the tactic of united front from below is easily traced in the statements of the Comintern and of the CPUSA in the magazines *Communist International (CI), The Communist (TC),* and *The Party Organizer (TPO).* For a general discussion of these policies, see *CI:* editorial, "The Competition of the Masses for the Revolution," 6, no. 23 (n.d., but probably fall 1929): 912; editorial, "On the Broad Road to Winning the Masses: The Forthcoming Fifth Congress of the RILD," 7, no. 6 (n.d., 1930?): 61-64; O. Piatnitsky, "All Sections of the CI Can and Must Become Really Mass Parties," 7, no. 11 (n.d.): 215-26; O. Bever, "Organizational Tasks at a New Stage," 8, no. 8 (May 1, 1931): 241-46.

11. The seriousness of this problem was recognized early by the Comintern. It was analyzed in detail by O. Piatnitsky, an organizational and political specialist. See "The Bolshevization of the Communist Parties of the Capitalist Countries by Means of Overcoming Social Democratic Traditions," *CI* 9, nos. 8-9 (May 15, 1932): 251-72. Several months later a much more specific criticism of the American Party was made. See J. Tsirul, "How the American Communist Party Carries Out Self-Criticism and Controls Fulfillment of Decisions," *CI* 9, no. 15 (August 15, 1932): 512-19.

12. For these Party membership figures, see Earl Browder's report to the Eighth National Convention, *DW,* April 14, 1934, pp. 3 ff. Also see *DW,* February 15, 1934, p. 4.

13. On fluctuation and the problems of retaining members, see the lead editorial "Why a Recruiting Drive Now?" *TPO* 5, nos. 9-10 (September-October 1932): 2-3. On the effort to organize the key industries, see the editorial "Every Factory a Fortress of Communism," *TPO* 4, nos. 8-9 (September-October 1931): 1-5. The editorial offers this data: there are 652 street nuclei and Party groups, of which 75 are shop nuclei representing a mere 4 percent of the Party membership–i.e., fewer than 500 workers are in shop nuclei. Jack Stachal's report to the CC in May 1935 reviews Party membership since the issuance of the Open Letter. He reports membership at 31,000, with 40 percent listed as unemployed. There are 9,800 union members. There are 4,668 workers in heavy industries and 7,173 in light. There are 500 shop nuclei and 1,650 street cells. See "Organizational Problems of the Party," *TC* 14, no. 7 (July 1935): 625-40. Also revealing is the New York State membership report for May 1935. The membership was 9,363, with 159 shop nuclei in basic industries representing 978 workers. There were 5,397 members working, and of these 53 percent were members of unions and 17 percent of these were in the A.F.L. Overall in New York the membership breakdown was: 10 percent in basic industries, 50 percent in light industries, 25 percent white collar and professional, and 15 percent housewives, unskilled workers, and students. See Max Steinberg, "Achievements and Tasks of the New York District (Organizational Report Submitted to the New York Party District Conference, February 23-24, 1935)," *TC* 14, no. 5 (May 1935): 444-58.

14. "An Open Letter," (New York, 1933), p. 4. That this contradiction dominated

the party discussions is clear from a perusal of *The Communist:* Earl Browder, "Next Task of the CP of the USA," 9, nos. 11-12 (November-December 1930): 972-78; Earl Browder, "Report of the Political Committee to the Twelfth CC Plenum, CPUSA, November 22, 1930," 10, no. 1 (January 1931): 7-31; Jack Stachal, "Coming Struggles and Lessons in Strike Strategy," 10, no. 3 (March 1931): 204-13; John Williamson, "The Party Nucleus: A Factor in the Class Struggle," 10, no. 5 (May 1931): 424-32; "To the Masses–To the Shops! Organize the Masses! Extracts from the Report of the Political Bureau to the CC, Thirteenth Plenum, CPUSA, August 21," 10, no. 9 (October 1931): 797-817; the April and May 1932 issues, devoted specifically to the resolutions of the Fourteenth Plenum of the CC (April 1, 1932) on the questions of working the factories.

15. "An Open Letter," pp. 20-21.
16. Ibid., pp. 13-17.
17. Ibid., pp. 17-18.
18. On the evaluation of the implementation of the Open Letter, See *The Communist:* Jack Stachal, "Lessons of the Economic Struggles and the Worker in the Trade Union," 13, no. 3 (March 1934): 272-301; editorial, "The Present Situation and the Tasks of the CPUSA (Resolution of the Eigth National Convention, Cleveland, Ohio, April 2-8, 1934)," 13, no. 5 (May 1934): 430-55; Jack Stachal, "Some Problems in Our Trade Union Work," 13, no. 6 (June 1934): 524-35; editorial, "In the Midst of Great Historic Battle," 13, no. 8 (August 1934): 739-50; and Earl Browder, "Report to the CC Meeting of CPUSA January 15-18, 1934," 14, no. 3 (March 1935): 195-216–an overview of trade union work since the Open Letter and the announcement of the end of independent Trade Union Unity League organizing and a return to the A.F.L. See also Jack Stachal, "How Are the Convention Decisions Being Carried into Life?" *TPO* 7, no. 7 (July 1934): 1.
19. Earl Browder, "The Situation in the United States of America," *TCI* 11, no. 2 (January 15, 1934): 75-80.
20. B. Sherman, "The Eighth Convention of the CP of the U.S.A. and Some Conclusions," *TCI* 11, no. 12 (June 20, 1934): 390-94.
21. The Comintern was especially concerned with the circulation and quality of the *DW,* and as part of the Open Letter program it evaluated its performance: "Review of the 'Daily Worker' USA (In Order of Checking Up the Carrying Out of the Tasks Put before the CP of the U.S.A. by the ECCI)," *CI* 10, no. 21 (November 1, 1933): 726-40; and "Review of the 'Party Life' Section of the American, Daily Worker' from October 22 to November 2, 1933," *TCI* 11, no. 1 (January 1, 1934): 33-36. Earl Browder, "New Steps in the United Front," *TC* 14, no. 11 (November 1935): 1009. This was his report on the Seventh Congress delivered to an open meeting of the CP, District 2, Madison Square Garden, on October 3, 1935. This discussion is continued in his report to the CC plenum in November: "The United Front: The Key to Our New Tactical Orientation," *TC* 14, no. 12 (December 1935): 1075-1129.
22. On references to separate party identity, see Earl Browder, "The Communists in the United Front," *TC* 16, no. 7 (July 1937): 594-627 and his "Struggle for the People's Front in the U.S.," *TCI* 14, no. 6 (June 1937): 391-96; also see William Z. Foster, "Political Leadership and Party Building," *TC* 16, no. 7 (July 1937): 628-46, and Foster's two reports on the A.F.L. to the Comintern: "The Convention of the American Federation of Labor," *TCI* 14, no. 1 (January 1937): 45-50, and "The Renaissance of the American Trade Union Movement," *TCI* 14, no. 6 (June 1937): 397-402.
23. James R. Prickett, "Anti-Communism and Labor History," *Industrial Relations* 13 (October 1974): 220-43.
24. James R. Prickett, "Communists and the Communist Issue in the American

Labor Movement, 1920–1950," (Ph.D. dissertation, UCLA, 1975), p. 27.
25. Ibid., pp. 35-36.
26. Ibid., p. 42.
27. Ibid., p. 43.
28. Ibid., p. 245.
29. Ibid., p. 456.
30. Organization-Education Commission of the CC, "The January 1938 Registration: An Analysis and Conclusion," *TPO* 11, no. 6 (June 1938): 1-6. The trend reflected in this large report can also be seen in data submitted from California and New York: "Party Organization in California," *TPO* 10, no. 7 (July 1937): 6; and Max Steinberg, Organizing Secretary for New York reported membership at 30,000 in 860 branches with 9,883 women, 1,841 Negroes, 15,115 union members, and 11,149 industrial workers. But fluctuation was enormous. In the period 1936-38 20,716 people were recruited but 10,147 were lost; "Rooting the Party Among the Masses in New York," *TC* 17, no. 9 (September 1938): 829-41.
31. See Foster, *Toward* pp. 345-49. Also see these articles in the *TPO:* "Control Tasks on Building the Party and the Circulation of Our Press," 10, nos. 3-4 (March-April 1937): 1-8; Charles Krumbein, "Some Lessons from the Party Registration," 10, no. 5 (May 1937): 1-4; David Armstrong, "Work among Professional People," 10, no. 5 (May 1937): 25-29–this is the only case history on professionals or intellectuals in the Party press; A. Landy, "Key Problems in Our Educational Work," 11, no. 2 (February 1938): 1-6.
32. Clarence Hathaway, "Building the Democratic Front," *TC* 17, no. 5 (May 1938), 404-9.
33. Gene Dennis, "Some Questions Concerning the Democratic Front," *TC* 17, no. 6 (June 1938): 535 and 538.
34. Earl Browder, "Some Remarks on the Twentieth Anniversary of the CPUSA," *TC* 18, no. 9 (September 1939): 803 and 798-802.
35. William Z. Foster, "The Human Element in Mass Agitation," *TC* 18, no. 4 (April 1939): 352.

7: THE PROLETARIAN PHASE IN AMERICA

1. Walter B. Rideout, *The Radical Novel in the United States, 1900-1954: Some Interrelations of Literature and Society* (New York, 1956), pp. 144-50, 165-60, 226-34, and 241-54.
2. Ibid., pp. 248-49; emphasis added.
3. Joseph Freeman, intro to *Proletarian Literature, in the United States: An Anthology,* (New York, 1935) p. 19. For checklists of proletarian/revolutionary fiction printed at the height of the proletarian phase, see Granville Hicks, "Revolutionary Literature of 1934," *NM* 14, no. 1 (January 1, 1935): 36-38, and "American Writers Look Left," *NM* 20, no. 1 (June 30, 1936): 24-26.
4. Many of these statements have already been discussed or noted. But several others are also worth citing: 1. On the variety of critical views at the high point of proletarian literature, see the section on literary criticism in *Proletarian Literature,* pp. 323-79, and the speeches of Cowley, Frank, Conroy, and Seaver at the First Writers' Congress in Henry Hart, ed., *American Writers' Congress* (New York, 1935). 2. For what everyone agrees is the most "left" analysis, see E. A. Schachner, "Revolutionary Literature in the United States Today," *Windsor Quarterly* (Vermont) 2(spring 1934): 27-64. 3. For the best statement by the *Partisan Review* group prior to the schism, see Wallace Phelps and Philip Rahv, "Problem and Perspective in Revolutionary Literature," *PR* 1, no. 3 (June-July 1934): 3-10; this essay was reprinted in Freeman as "Recent Problems of Revolutionary Literature,"

pp. 367-73. 4. On the controversy sparked by James T. Farrell's *A Note on Literary Criticism* (New York, 1936), see Isidor Schneider's review "Sectarianism on the Right," *NM* 19, no. 13 (June 23, 1936): 23-25, and the ensuing debate throughout the summer in the magazine. 5. Gold's comments are scattered, but see his brief remarks to the First Writers' Congress in Hart, p. 16, and his columns in *DW* from mid-April to mid-May 1935. See also his "Migratory Intellectuals," *NM* 21, no. 12 (December 15, 1936): 27-29, and "Notes on the Cultural Front," *NM* 25, no. 11 (December 7, 1937): 1-5. 6. Hicks revised *The Great Tradition* in 1935 to include the rise of proletarian literature.

5. Rideout, p. 227, and James B. Gilbert, *Writers and Partisans: A History of Literary Radicalism in America* (New York, 1968), p. 122.

6. On circulation, see *NM* 14, no. 1 (January 1, 1935): 9. And on the proletarian magazines, see Orrick Johns, "The John Reed Clubs Meet," *NM* 13, no. 15 (October 30, 1934): 25-26.

7. On the expanse of published and produced revolutionary literature, see note 3 above. Also see the important essay by Joseph Freeman, "Ivory Towers—White and Red," *NM* 12, no. 11 (September 11, 1934): 24.

8. Freeman, "Ivory Towers," pp. 21-23.

9. A. B. Magil, "Pity and Terror," *NM* 8, no. 5 (December, 1932): 18-19.

10. Freeman, "Ivory Towers," p. 23.

11. Joseph North, ed., *New Masses: An Anthology of the Rebel Thirties* (New York, 1969), p. 25.

12. A conversation with the author, August 14, 1976.

8: THE AESTHETICS OF THE POPULAR FRONT

1. John Dos Passos, *The Big Money,* pp. 413-14, in *U.S.A.* (Boston, Sentry ed., 1960).

2. "Stewart Elected Head of Writers' Congress," *DW,* June 8, 1937, p. 3.

3. For a positive review, see Isidor Schneider, *NM* 20, no. 7 (August 11, 1936): 40-41. On Dos Passos's break with the CP, see Melvin Landsberg, *Dos Passos' Path to U.S.A.: A Political Biography* (Boulder, Colo., 1972), pp. 180 and passim. On the tenderness with which the left treated him even after the fracas at Madison Square Garden, see *NM* 10, no. 8 (March 6, 1934): 8-9.

4. Mike Gold's column "Change The World: What about Dos Passos?" *DW,* July 31, 1937, p. 7.

5. Quoted in Townsend Ludington, ed., *The Fourteenth Chronicle: Letters and Diaries of John Dos Passos* (Boston, 1973), p. 514. For a recent, sophisticated discussion of Dos Passos's turn to the right, see John P. Diggins, *Up from Communism: Conservative Odysseys in American Intellectual History* (New York, 1975), pp. 1-14 and 74-117.

6. Granville Hicks, "The Mood and Tenses of John Dos Passos," *NM* 27, no. 5 (April 26, 1938), 22-23.

7. Mike Gold, "Migratory Intellectuals," *NM* 21, no. 12 (December 15, 1936): 28.

8. Ibid., p. 29.

9. Hicks's review and the exchange of letters are reprinted in Jack Alan Robbins, ed., *Granville Hicks in the New Masses* (Port Washington, N.Y., 1974), pp. 382-406.

10. Arnold Shukotoff, "Proletarian Short Stories," *NM* 30, no. 2 (January 3, 1939): 23.

11. Samuel Sillen, "The Funeral Is Off Again," *NM* 29, no. 7 (November 8, 1938): 23-24.

12. Samuel Sillen, "The People, Yes," *NM* 31, no. 11 (June 6, 1939): 22-23.

13. Joshua Kunitz, "In Defense of a Term," *NM* 28, Literary Supplement (July 12, 1938): 145. Lowenfels's letter is reprinted in the essay.

14. Ibid., p. 147.

15. Ibid., p. 146.

16. Mike Gold, "Notes on the Cultural Front," *NM* 25, no. 11 Literary Supplement (December 7, 1937): 1-5. See James T. Farrell, "The Last Writers' Congress: An Interim Report on Its Results," *Saturday Review of Literature,* 16, no. 6 (June 5, 1937): 10 ff. Gold's article led off the new literary supplement edited by Gold, Hicks, Gregory, and Kunitz, which would try to provide an outlet for original writing and essays during the new popular front period. For the announcement of the new monthly supplement, see *NM* 25, no. 6 (November 2, 1937): 2.
17. Gold, "Notes," 5.
18. Ibid.
19. "The Fight for Popular-Priced Books," *NM* 33, no. 6 (October 21, 1939): 18.
20. Ibid., pp. 25-26.

9: MARXIST AESTHETIC THEORY

1. Lee Baxandall, ed., *Marxism and Aesthetics: A Selective Annotated Bibliography* (New York, 1968).
2. Lee Baxandall and Stefan Morawski, eds., *Marx and Engels on Literature and Art* (St. Louis, Mo., 1973).
3. Engels's letter to Joseph Bloch (1890) clearly shows the persistence of this problem. Howard Selsam and Henry Martel, eds., *Reader in Marxist Philosophy* (New York, 1963), pp. 205-6:

Marx and I are ourselves partly to blame for the fact that younger writers sometimes lay more stress on the economic side than is due to it. We had to emphasize this main principle in opposition to our adversaries, who denied it, and we had not always the time, the place or the opportunity to allow the other elements involved in the interaction to come into their rights. But when it was a case of presenting a section of history, that is, of practical application, the thing was different and there no error was possible. Unfortunately, however, it happens only too often that people think that they fully understood a theory and can apply it without much ado from the moment they have mastered its main principles, and those not always correctly.

4. Karl Marx, in *Marx and Engels: Selected Works* (New York, 1969), pp. 181-85.
5. Marx and Engels, in Selsam and Martel, p. 199.
6. Ibid., p. 190:

Men are the producers of their conceptions, ideas, etc.—real active men, as they are conditioned by a definite development of their productive forces and of the intercourse corresponding to these, up to the furthest forms. Consciousness can never be anything else than conscious existence, and the existence of men is their actual life process. . . . Morality, religion, metaphysics, all the rest of ideology and theircorresponding forms of consciousness, thus no longer retain the semblance of independence. They have no history, no development; but men, developing their material production and their material intercouse, alter, along with this real existence, their thinking. Life is not determined by consciousness, but consciousness by life.

And from Engels's letter to F. Mehring (1893) in *Selected Works,* p. 700: "Ideology is a process accomplished by the so called thinker consciously, it is true, but with a false consciousness. And I cannot exempt many of the more recent Marxists' from this reproach, for the most wonderful rubbish has been produced from this quarter, too."

7. Baxandall and Morawski, p. 47. The essay under analysis here first appeared in a shorter form as "The Aesthetic Views of Marx and Engels," *Journal of Aesthetics and Art Criticism* (spring 1970), pp. 301-14. For all that Marx ever had to say about literature, see S. S. Prawer, *Karl Marx and World Literature* (Oxford, 1976).

8. Another example of this problem is seen in an introductory essay to a competent college anthology, Berel Lang and Forrest Williams, eds., *Marxism and Art: Writings in Aesthetics and Criticism* (New York, 1972).
9. Parts one and five will be treated together; see below, pp. 105-7.
10. Baxandall and Morawski, p. 5. On the first point, he argues for a vision of continuity from early to late Marx, rejecting both Louis Althusser (*Pour Marx*) for his split of Marx's development into phases—humanist and scientific—and Robert C. Tucker (*Philosophy and Myth in Karl Marx*) for his view of Marx as a prophet and utopian.
11. Baxandall and Morawski, pp. 7-8. Morawski will cite the treatments of Eugene Sue's *Les Mystères de Paris* and Ferdinand LaSalle's *Franz von Sickingen* as prime textual sources for dominant themes.
12. The academic debates usually focus on the differences between Marx's early humanism and his later revolutionary politics.
13. Baxandall and Morawski, p. 8.
14. Ibid., p. 9.
15. Ibid., pp. 9-12. Despite the obtuseness of the synopsis, I believe it to be a fair rendering of this section.
16. Ibid., pp. 7 and 11. It should be noted at this point that the emphasis on continuity from Hegel to Marx and on what Morawski calls the other "idiogenetic" sources impinging on the aesthetic ideas of Marx and Engels is specifically a revision of Mikhail Lifshitz, *The Philosophy of Art and Karl Marx* (New York, 1938) and an attack on Lifshitz's effort to separate Marx from Hegel.
17. The source materials from Marx and Engels are arranged in the text on pp. 51-154 to correspond with Morawski's analysis in part four of the essay.
18. Baxandall and Morawski, p. 14 and pp. 13-18. Again this summary is abstract, but it does accurately reflect the entire section.
19. Ibid., pp. 18-19, p. 22, and pp. 18-25.
20. Ibid., p. 30 and pp. 25-30.
21. Ibid., p. 30, p. 33, and pp. 30-35.
22. Ibid., pp. 35-39.
23. Lang and Williams also argue that Marxist interpretations of art must be given academic respectability. See Lang and Williams, pp. 1-9.
24. Baxandall and Morawski, pp. 24, 32, and 38.
25. Ibid., pp. 40-44 and 45.
26. See part one of Morawski's essay "A Note on the Texts and Previous Interpretations," pp. 3-4.
27. Lifshitz, pp. 75, 78, 79, and 84. Interestingly, Morawski does not acknowledge the stress which Lifshitz places on the class nature of art-a point Morawski often underestimates. Also, Morawski does not acknowledge the predictive quality of the Lifshitz analysis.
28. The third mistaken approach is directed toward the work of Andrew N. Jezuitow, especially *Woprosi rjealizma w estjetike Marxa i Engelsa* (Moscow, 1963).
29. Georgij M. Fridlender, *K. Marx i F. Engels i woprosi litjeraturi* (Moscow, 1962), p. 10 and pp. 1-9.
30. Pavel S. Trofimov, *Otsherki istorii marksistokoj estetiki* (Moscow, 1963), p. 5.
31. Baxandall and Morawski, p. 46.
32. It is important to note that he is but one of several thinkers whose writings might be classified as forming the "central" or "classic" texts on aesthetics (or other superstructure problems). It is safe to conclude that the following works are most consistently cited: N. Bukharin, *Historical Materialism: A System of Sociology,* 3rd. ed., (New York, 1965); V. I. Lenin, "Party Organization and Party Literature" (1905) in *Works* 8, (Moscow, 1931): 386; Mao Tse-Tung, *On Literature and Art* (Peking, 1960); J. Stalin, *Marxism and Linguistics,* (New York, 1951) in Bruce Franklin, ed., *The Essential Stalin: Major Theoretical Writings 1905-1952* (New York, 1972); and Leon Trotsky, *Literature and Revolution* (Ann Arbor, Mich., 1971).

33. Lee Baxandall, "Marxism and Aesthetics: A Critique of the Contribution of George Plekhanov," *Journal of Aesthetics and Art Criticism* 25 (spring 1967): 267-79.

34. George Plekhanov, *Art and Social Life* (London, 1935), edited by Andrew Rothstein, contains the essays "Letters without Address" (translated by Eric Hartley) and "French Dramatic Literature and French Eighteenth-Century Painting from the Sociological Standpoint." *Art and Society* (New York, 1936), translated by Alfred Goldstein with an introduction by Granville Hicks, contains the important essay "Art and Society." Another important collection of his theoretical writings is *Fundamental Problems of Marxism* (New York, 1969), which also includes the famous essays "The Materialist Conception of History" (1897) and "The Role of the Individual in History" (1898).

35. Plekhanov *Art and Social Life*, pp. 95 and 109.

36. See *Art and Social Life*, pp. 164-65, for Plekhanov's conclusions based on research into French literature; see Rothstein's introduction (p. 12) for further analysis.

37. Plekhanov, *Art and Society*, p. 37–from the title essay.

38. Ibid., p. 48.

39. Ibid., p. 80.

40. Ibid., p. 48.

41. Ibid., pp. 87-88.

42. Ibid., p. 66.

43. Plekhanov, *Art and Social Life*, p. 20.

44. Harold Swayze, *Political Control of Literature in the USSR, 1946-1959* (Cambridge, Mass., 1962), pp. 5-6.

45. Ibid., p. 16.

46. Plekhanov also suggests a use for art: ". . . Plekhanov linked the possibility of high artistic achievement to a definite world view and a particular cause, and he tended to regard the liberation of the proletariat as the value of values, the ultimate criterion for evaluating everything" (Swayze, p. 7).

47. For the expanse and variety of approaches, see the Baxandall bibliography and the documents cited in the Lang and Williams anthology.

48. Ernst Fischer, *The Necessity of Art: A Marxist Approach* (London, 1963), pp. 13-14.

49. Ibid., pp. 33-36.

50. Ibid., pp. 40 and 46-47.

51. The excerpts on sociology and art appear in the Lang and Williams anthology, and citations will be from that source.

52. The clearest example of such critics and their attack on the sociological approach appears in René Wellek and Austin Warren, *Theory of Literature* (New York, 3rd ed., 1956), especially their chapter on "Literature and Society," pp. 94-109, and pp. 29, 73, and 238.

53. Lang and Williams, p. 272. At this point it is perhaps wise to pay tribute to the quintessential work on the sociology of knowledge, Karl Mannheim's *Ideology and Utopia: An Introduction to the Sociology of Knowledge* (New York, 1936). The work should be seen in part as a specific critique of Marxism as a form of ideology.

54. Lang and Williams, p. 275.

55. Ibid., p. 279.

56. See ibid., p. 246; quoted from Lucien Goldmann, *Pour une sociologie du roman* (Paris, 1964). The method of his "scientific" approach is also outlined in this work.

57. See also Goldmann, *Sciences humaines et philosophie* (Paris, 1952) and his *Recherches dialectiques* (Paris, 1958).

58. Lucien Goldmann, *The Hidden God: A Study of Tragic Vision in the Pensées of Pascal and the Tragedies of Racine* (New York, 1964, trans. Philip Thody), pp. 19

and 20. See the entire first chapter, "The Whole and the Parts," for a discussion of such issues as dialectics, empiricism, the relation of ideas to social groups, science applied to humanistic studies, etc.

59. Lang and Williams, p. 250.

60. Goldmann, p. 7.

61. Frederic Jameson, *Marxism and Form: Twentieth-Century Dialectical Theories of Literature* (Princeton, N.J., 1971). Jameson's twofold purpose is to introduce to the American academic community the French and German Marxist dialectical traditions and to provide his own theoretical approach to the study of literature based on an analysis of these critics. What makes Jameson of interest is an approach which attempts a critique of specific writers connected to an analysis of the basic assumptions of Marxism from which he constructs an aesthetic. Obviously, it is a sharply different approach from the one I offer. Jameson reviews T. W. Adorno, Walter Benjamin, Herbert Marcuse, Friedrich Schiller, Ernst Bloch, George Lukacs, and Jean-Paul Sartre, concluding with a hundred-page essay detailing his theory of a dialectical approach to literature.

62. Jameson, pp. x-xi.

63. Ibid., pp. xviii-xix.

64. Ibid., p. 307. His essay is entitled "Towards Dialectical Criticism."

65. Ibid., pp. 402-3.

66. Ibid., p. 416.

67. Ibid., pp. 372-73.

68. Ibid., p. 319. And see pp. 312ff. for an example of such a separable unit—i.e., romantic sensibility as it develops and changes in Baudelaire, Swinburne, and Rimbaud.

69. Jameson, p. 328.

70. Ibid., pp. 331-32. And interestingly, in a later section, Jameson justifies Marxist criticism which shifts from the literary to the socioeconomic or historical element ". . . as an enlargement structurally inherent in such criticism, as an intrinsic and indispensable moment in Marxist literary criticism, as a *form* of understanding" (p. 378). Apparently, when discussing Hegel Jameson sees a dialectical connection in the relationship between intrinsic and extrinsic issues, but when discussing Marx this relationship simply becomes a necessary outgrowth. This is an apparent contradiction which Jameson never resolves.

71. This vision of the relationship is based on the work of Sidney Hook. (See Jameson pp. 365-66 and especially note 30 for his indebtedness to Hook.)

72. Jameson, pp. 322-26.

73. Ibid., p. 336.

74. It must also be noted that Jameson is offering some very sharp criticism of Marxism. See pp. 375, 359, and 361-62.

75. Ibid., p. 333.

76. Ibid., p. xi.

BIBLIOGRAPHY

This is not meant to be a thorough analysis of every source cited or consulted. For a detailed illumination of sources, see the notes and bibliography in the author's "The CPUSA's Approach to Literature in the 1930s: Socialist Realism and the American Party's 'Line' on Literature" (Ph.D. dissertation, Rutgers University, 1977).

THE CPUSA AND CULTURE IN THE 1930s

There are three central studies which must form the basis of any reevaluation of Communism and culture in the 1930s. While often presenting valuable data, these secondary sources have a fundamental anti-Communist bias which limits their usefulness and validity. From this perspective the least objectionable work is Walter B. Rideout, *The Radical Novel in the United States, 1900-1954: Some Inter-relations of Literature and Society* (New York, 1956). He is primarily concerned with defining and categorizing proletarian fiction as a literary genre. The attempt by Communists to lead this literary movement, Rideout believes, is reflected in literary debates and controversies and in the organizational changes imposed by the Party—though he never thoroughly discusses the Party line. He sees throughout the thirties the gradual subjugation of literature to politics, noting the decline of proletarian fiction as the post-1935 united front expands. In Rideout's view, proletarian fiction, as a literary genre, ends with the shattering of the united front.

Daniel Aaron's *Writers on The Left* (New York, 1965), is a far more ambitious text and far more contemptuous of Communism. It is a study of the American cultural environment as he examines why certain writers and intellectuals turned to the CPUSA, why they stayed such a short time, and why they broke so sharply. The anti-Communism in Aaron is clear: the Party's attempts to politicize both the writers and the literature are attacked. Its heavy hand, rigid bureaucratism, and subservience to the Soviet Union fail to hold the intellectuals who have shifted left as a "gut response" to the harshness of the depression. The intellectuals, Aaron believes, wore the "red shirt" of Communism as a symbol of their disgust with America. He suggests that this failure to hold the intellectuals as converts to Communism is representative of the failure of Communist ideology.

The third text in this essential group is Irving Howe and Lewis Coser, *The American Communist Party: A Critical History, 1919-1957* (Boston, 1957). Too often accepted uncritically as a definitive history, it is tendentious, vitriolic, and shallow; this is probably explained by Howe's Trotskyist political and intellectual affiliations. In part, this study tries to demonstrate how the extensive cultural apparatus of the Party under direct control of Moscow poisoned the intellectual and cultural life of the country.

Perhaps the most important dissenting view and the least anti-Communist scholarly analysis is Joseph Starobin's retrospective chapter on the thirties, "Remembrances of Things Past", in *American Communism in Crisis 1943-1957* (Cambridge, Mass., 1972). He suggests that efforts on the cultural front were rather minimal and best seen as offshoots of the trade union movement and the united front strategy. This is one of the few scholarly works that make a serious attempt to explain Party failures while recognizing positive achievements in practice. Starobin's analysis is an important corrective and should not be overlooked, even though it is focused on the post–World War 2 era.

A sympathetic understanding of the Party as an activist Communist movement requires a careful review of the Party press, reflecting as it does the Party's public activity. During this period the best overview of the day-to-day activity is in the *Daily Worker*. It is unwieldy as a research tool, since it has no index, but there is no other source that provides the expanse and depth of Party work. It is also a powerful documentary record of the Party's achievement. Unfortunately, it is far too often disregarded or dismissed by scholars. The theoretical bases and organizational decisions are presented in *The Communist* and *The Party Organizer*, and the ties to the international movement and the Soviet Union are detailed in the *Communist International* and *International Press Correspondence*.

Obviously, the cultural work of the Party is best revealed in the *New Masses,* especially as it grew from a minor radical literary journal of

6,000 circulation to the most important political and cultural magazine on the left with a circulation of 30,000. The significant literary/political debates on the cultural front cannot be thoroughly understood or evaluated without consulting the magazines. Also, many published cultural commentaries—for example, Granville Hick's attempt at a Marxist literary history, *The Great Tradition* (New York, 1933 and 1935), James T. Farrell's literary attack against the Party, *A Note on Literary Criticism* (New York, 1936), Joseph Freeman's sharp personal narrative, *An American Testament* (London, 1938), and Mike Gold's denouncement of Trotskyist intellectuals, *The Hollow Men* (New York, 1941)—should not be read in isolation from this journal.

Most of the important political pronouncements and speeches are contained in the Party press. By way of political explanation, Earl Browder's *What Is Communism?* (New York, 1935) and *The People's Front* (New York, 1938) are crucial. William Z. Foster's *Toward Soviet America* (New York, 1932) is also necessary. While often tendentious and inaccurate, Foster's *History of the Communist Party of the United States* (New York, 1968) offers some profound retrospective insights. Mike Gold is perhaps the least appreciated Communist writer, critic, and commentator. He is often deprecated for his political inflexibility, but his understanding of the practical aspects of Communism in America is profound and most clearly revealed in his *Daily Worker* column "Change The World." See also Mike Gold, *The Mike Gold Reader: From the Writings of Mike Gold* (New York, 1954). On his ability as a writer, see *Jews without Money* (1930) and Mike Folsom, ed., *Mike Gold: A Literary Anthology* (New York, 1972).

The best collection of proletarian literature is still Granville Hicks et al., eds., *Proletarian Literature in the United States* (New York, 1935). For other literary selections chosen as representative of the proletarian literary phase by important participants, see Joseph North, ed., *New Masses: An Anthology of the Rebel Thirties* (New York, 1969) and Jack Conroy, and Curt Johnson, eds., *Writers in Revolt: The Anvil Anthology, 1933-1940* (New York, 1973). For a critical, historical, and aesthetic evaluation of the proletarian phenomenon, see the collection of essays in David Madden, ed., *Proletarian Writers of the Thirties* (Carbondale, Ill., 1968).

SOVIET SOCIALIST REALISM

Recently there has been a significant development in research on culture in the Soviet Union during the early Stalin period. Sheila Fitzpatrick, ed., *Cultural Revolution in Russia, 1928-1931* (Bloomington,

Ind., 1978) is a first attempt to break down much of the cold war mythology regarding both Stalin and totalitarianism. However, the post-World War 2 interpretations of socialist realism emanated primarily from the academic centers of Soviet studies in America where the still universally accepted notion of Stalin as dictator was packaged for academic circles. Typical examples are Robert C. Tucker, *Stalin as Revolutionary, 1879-1929: A Study in History and Personality* (New York, 1973) and Adam Ulam, *Stalin: The Man and His Era* (New York, 1973); the most famous hostile biographies, however, come from an earlier opposition—Boris Souvarine, *Stalin: A Critical Survey of Bolshevism* (New York, 1939) and Isaac Deutscher, *Stalin* (London, 1949).

Gleb Struve's, *Russian Literature under Lenin and Stalin, 1917-1953* (Norman, Okla., 1970) is exemplary of texts which align socialist realism with the dictator hypothesis, thus, the imposition of socialist realism was one part of the program to increase control and to insure censorship in all social and political affairs marking Stalin's rise to power. Such an interpretation assumes that this was a deliberate regimentation of literature and art to force obeisance to the political line of the Party; that with the aid of Stalin's political henchmen unwilling writers were compelled to participate in the single Writers' Union. This approach is also popular with non-Marxist social scientists writing during the cold war period and who treat the entire Stalin era in totalitarian terms. Such ahistoricism is best seen in Harold Swayze, *Political Control of Literature in the U.S.S.R.* (Cambridge, Mass., 1962).

The Marxist defenders of socialist realism argue that it is a world-wide literary phenomenon reflecting the emergence of socialism and its positive influence on art. They suggest that it developed from the convergence of realism in art and Marxism-Leninism in politics, with the Soviet Union providing artistic leadership in the 1930s. For the most sympathetic description of Soviet literary policy and its background, see C. V. James, *Soviet Socialist Realism: Origins and Theory* (New York, 1973). James has also translated a collection of essays and critical articles on this issue representing current Soviet attitudes, *Socialist Realism in Literature and Art: A Collection of Articles* (Moscow, 1971). For an earlier Soviet view, see M. Gorky, *Literature and Life: A Selection from the Writings of Maxim Gorky* (New York, 1946).

For Marxists "Stalinism" is also a problem. In line with the process of de-Stalinization after Khrushchev's secret speech, they see the excesses of the 1930s as part of an aberration of Marxism prompted by the cult of personality. Georg Lukacs, perhaps the most famous Marxist literary critic, shifts his view of socialist realism from a supportive position in the 1930s to sharp criticism of "Stalinism" in the 1950s. For his early analysis, see "On Socialist Realism" *International Literature* 4 (1939): 87-96. For the later critical discussion, see *The Meaning of Contemporary Realism* (London, 1963), especially the essay "Critical Realism and Socialist Realism" written in 1956, and *Solzhenitsyn* (Cambridge, Mass., 1971).

The two non-Marxist monographs which discuss RAPP and Soviet socialist realism are marred by overt anti-Communism; they align with the prevailing hostile interpretations of the Soviet Union during the Stalin era. On RAPP, see Edward J. Brown, *The Proletarian Episode in Russian Literature, 1928-1932* (New York, 1953); extending and reinterpreting Brown's analysis into a history of the origins of socialist realism is Herman Ermolaev, *Soviet Literary Theories: 1917-1934, The Genesis of Socialist Realism* (Berkeley, 1963). As a corrective, see Sheila Fitzpatrick, "Cultural Revolution As Class War," in *Cultural Revolution in Russia, 1928-1931*, and also her "Culture and Politics under Stalin: A Reappraisal," *Slavic Review* 35 (June 1976): 211-31.

For a reconsideration of Stalin, see Bruce Franklin, ed., *The Essential Stalin: Major Theoretical Writings, 1905-1952* (New York, 1972). Read critically, *History of the Communist Party of the Soviet Union* (1939) and "Road to Revolution III," *Progressive Labor* 8 (November 1971): 8-25 offer insight into the historical development of Communism and Stalin's role.

The American response to the changes in the Soviet Union are best seen in the literary journals the *New Masses, The Literature of World Revolution,* and *International Literature.*

Max Eastman's *Artists in Uniform: A Study of Literature and Bureaucratism* (New York, 1934), a vindictive and inaccurate essay, argued that the Kharkov Conference was the beginning of American acceptance of Soviet orders on the literary front. Most of the standard secondary sources have accepted Eastman's charges, though with different levels of hysteria. See Daniel Aaron, *Writers on the Left* as a representative example, and also see Daniel Aaron (moderator), "Thirty Years Later: Memories of the First American Writers' Congress," *American Scholar* 35 (1965): 495-516—for his misrepresentation of the chronology.

MARXIST AESTHETIC THEORY

My interest in Marxist aesthetic theory has its roots in the epistemology of Marxism—i.e., the method of dialectical materialism. It is my belief that the writings of Marx, Engels, and Lenin provide a necessary background to an understanding of this epistemology, but not a magic formula. This method is in my view a tool of analysis. It can be best reviewed in such works as F. Engels, *Anti-Dühring* (New York, 1939), *Dialectics of Nature* (New York, 1940), *Ludwig Feuerbach* (New York, 1941), and *Socialism, Utopian and Scientific* (New York, 1935), K. Marx *The Poverty of Philosophy* (Moscow, nd.), selections from *Capital*, vol. 1 (New York, 1947), and *The Eighteenth Brumaire of Louis Bonaparte* (New York, 1963), Marx and Engels, *The German Ideology* New York, 1942), and V.I. Lenin, *Materialism and Empirio Criticism* (Moscow 1937).

INDEX

145

150 / INDEX